The Illusion of Leadership

The Illusion of Leadership

Directing Creativity in Business and the Arts

Piers Ibbotson

palgrave
macmillan

First published 2008 by
PALGRAVE MACMILLAN

Palgrave Macmillan in the UK is an imprint of Macmillan Publishers Limited,
registered in England, company number 785998, of Houndmills, Basingstoke,
Hampshire RG21 6XS.

Palgrave Macmillan in the US is a division of St Martin's Press LLC,
175 Fifth Avenue, New York, NY 10010.

Palgrave Macmillan is the global academic imprint of the above companies
and has companies and representatives throughout the world.

Palgrave® and Macmillan® are registered trademarks in the United States,
the United Kingdom, Europe and other countries.

ISBN-13: 978–0–230–20199–6
ISBN-10: 0–230–20199–7

This book is printed on paper suitable for recycling and made from fully
managed and sustained forest sources. Logging, pulping and manufacturing
processes are expected to conform to the environmental regulations of the
country of origin.

A catalogue record for this book is available from the British Library.

A catalog record for this book is available from the Library of Congress.

10 9 8 7 6 5 4 3 2 1
17 16 15 14 13 12 11 10 09 08

Printed and bound in Great Britain by
Cromwell Press Ltd, Trowbridge, Wiltshire

CONTENTS

LIST OF FIGURES

Acknowledgments

Nothing comes from nothing. As I hope this book clearly states, all the things we make are made from other things. Nothing in this book is original except the way I have written it and the conjunctions I have made. I have, as all artists do, threaded together fragments of other people's ideas and perceptions and woven them into my own narrative. Where I can be reasonably sure of the source of an idea or argument I have referred to a book or books that I know laid out those ideas. In many places I have stated as my own, ideas which others may recognize. This may be forgetfulness or it may be coincidence. If it feels like plagiarism it may well be; but unconscious plagiarism. I have not made an exhaustive search of the literature; so much of what I say may be out there already, even if I may feel I have discovered it myself. I hope that anyone who feels their ideas have been appropriated will feel free to correct me and, I hope, forgive me. I know I stand on the shoulders of others – it's just that sometimes I can't quite remember their names.

Among those whose names I can recall are: Tom Lloyd, Lotte Darsø, Michael Davids, Iain Mangham, Mary Midgley, Colin Funk, David Honigmann, Diana Winstanley, Tim Stockil and Arts and Business, Kate Sinclair, Dan Milne, Iain Oag, Barbara Houseman, Cis Berry, Adrian Jackson, Max Stafford Clark, Captain Joe Kay, Toby Wilshire and Trestle Theater Company, Jane Hilberry. Without their direct or indirect contributions I would never have got this far. Most of the core ideas are from the work of Keith Johnstone and of Augusto Boal whose work I have admired and appropriated for many years.

PIERS IBBOTSON

Most leaders emerge by accident rather than intent, even the powerful and important ones, because most people don't want the job. Standing up in front of others and persuading them to do something can be difficult and even frightening. People will do it because there is something they want: not "power" in the abstract, but to make their fragmentary vision of a possible future happen in the world. They need people to help them co-create it, and they will gather as followers those who share their response to the fragment they have communicated. It needs only a few – twelve to twenty-five – and they begin to co-create like a theater ensemble, cascading their influence through a whole organization or society.

Leaders make their work in the world from what their followers make. We can be a passive audience to this process, or we can be actors; we can direct others or we can improvise alongside them. We can participate in the play of life however we choose – but we cannot *not* be in it. Leadership is co-created. It does not lie in one party or the other. It is an illusion in which we all participate. I have my own experience of being a leader, and that was mostly in the theater where the "leader of the creative process" is called a director. I like that word better. It makes it clear that in a group creative enterprise, where the outcome requires innovation, you need someone to give a direction to the creative work of the group. Directors in the theater do exactly that. They point out the direction that things need to go in.

I talk to many business leaders in the course of my work and I have noticed that when they are more relaxed – after a few drinks, perhaps – their success stories change and they begin to admit that rather than having made a successful company solely by dint of careful planning and consistent execution, they have benefited from an enormous amount of luck. Things happened that were unexpected or disastrous. Bad decisions led to failure which then revealed an opportunity that they hadn't been able to see before. The idea that they had a map with a location marked on it to which they led the company along a clearly marked route is an illusion. They were lucky, they bluffed, they had good people around them, they took a chance and it worked out. This process of guessing and reframing, of following a hunch and then scrabbling to consolidate when the hunch works out, is a process I recognize. It is the creative process – directing a group of people through a complex and uncertain place, following a fragmentary vision, and trying to make it solid as you go.

I have called this book *The Illusion of Leadership* because I made a surprising discovery when I became a theater director. Prior to my first attempts to direct, I had been an actor. I had been led by others. In the process of being directed I had always assumed that I was, at some level, being manipulated or coerced into doing what the director wanted. Only late in my career did I discover an interesting secret: the best directors did not know in detail what was going to happen in the play until they saw me do it. They didn't tell me what I should do because they didn't know. This ability to carry on being in charge and maintaining the trust of the company, when you do not and cannot know in detail how things will turn out, seems to me to be at the heart of creative leadership in business and the arts.

I believe that many people outside the arts misunderstand the creative process and the behaviors necessary to encourage creative teamwork. If the right culture were in place, innovation would not be an issue; the function of managers would be like the function of a director of a good ensemble: merely to select from the stream of invention and suggestion pouring from the group as they engage with the tasks they have in hand. That is not to say that these conditions never arise, rather that business does not seem to know how to get them or where in the organization they need to be encouraged.

The behaviors that are in place in many of the business environments I have experienced are the opposite of those required for group creativity. They come from an internalized belief in competitive individualism. A generation has grown up who believe that "There is no such thing as society;" "It's a dog-eat-dog world;" "Only the fit survive." But of course there is such as thing as society; dogs never eat dogs: they cooperate in packs; and "fit" means "most appropriate to the circumstances" not "fastest and most ruthless." These simplistic misapprehensions, borne to us on a tide of largely American films and business culture, supported by some dubious reinterpretations of Darwin, have been readily adopted by a generation who see their organizations as largely soulless and themselves as striving for material benefits and the adrenaline rush of successful competition (Sennett 1998, 2006).

People see their work as a place where they manifest their lifestyle and cultural values and have less and less interest in the actual products or effects of the organization. Many people go to work precisely for the battles and the triumphs and the money. Increasingly, they don't care about either the long-term survival of the organization or the utility or quality of its products. This is partly, I suspect, because there is a perception that some of those who own and run these organizations don't care either. They are engaged in another game altogether. A game of corporate gin rummy where there is the possibility of untold wealth from the manipulation of market sentiment and the cutting of deals. The net result is that there is no one directing the flows of energy and invention that are manifesting in the business world. There seems to be no end in view apart from a generalized faith in "freedom" and an internalized belief that people's core motives, indeed their very DNA, are selfish. This is capitalist freedom it means "freedom from," not "freedom to." It is the state of being without boundaries or constraints. It is a kind of directionless swamp of self-indulgence.

Creativity flourishes at the edges of things. It needs boundaries and it needs constraints. The world of business has been described to me as "amoral," as if our behavior there need not concern itself too much with ethics. There is an affinity with the idea of self-as-scientist rather than self-as-artist; that what is necessary for good business leadership is clarity, precision, measurability and emotional detachment. These qualities are not necessarily wrong, but they are not always appropriate to the business of getting good ideas out of people and implementing them. And they exclude consideration of the deeper values that people express through the work they do and the choices they make.

Management is not science, but art. It is art in the sense that it needs to be practiced with the full self: with heart, mind and soul aligned. In business it seems to me there is both a need for and fear of this mindset. What follows is intended to be of direct practical help in understanding, and getting better at, leading and managing people in any organizational context. It is about developing the artistic mindset and applying it outside the arts. It is about learning to manage the paradoxical tension between creativity and constraint, between serendipity and intention. How to encourage things to evolve in the way they need to.

Because the evidence is mounting that some of the products of the thriving capitalist economies are beginning to destroy both our health and our planet. We need, urgently, to go in another direction.

Running through the book, and intimately tied up with these issues, are questions about power and ethics, because as managers, leaders and workers in today's organizations we must hold on to our humanity at work and endeavor to act with principle, with passion and with integrity.

For the last ten years I have been reflecting on my twenty years' experience as a theater performer and director and applying it in other contexts. I have worked with a wide range of organizations, both commercial and state-run, from engineering to aggregates, from media to medicine. In all I have encountered assumptions and practices that to my surprise were radically different from those in the arts. This book is an attempt to explore some of these differences and show how ideas from the arts can be successfully applied to business and other organizations.

I have set down what I consider to be best practice among the many and varied artists I have worked with. But much of my core experience was with the Royal Shakespeare Company where I worked as an actor and then as an assistant director over a period of about fifteen years, so my approach is influenced by an older theater, one where language, dialog and poetry are central to the work. I come from working in a theater where the director as keeper of the vision and leader of the process is firmly established; where the ideas and techniques of ensemble theater, brought from Europe by pioneering figures such as Joan Littlewood, are firmly embedded in most companies.

In terms of the evolution of the theater crafts, directing is the new arrival; particularly where the director is elevated to the status of auteur, with both the responsibility and the power to stamp their creative vision on the work of a playwright. In the Shakespearean theater, the role of director was probably closer to that of stage manager or even producer, the craft of the actors and the writer being the central focus of the process. It was only in the twentieth century that the director began to ascend, alongside the film director, to the status of artist in their own right, with the work of the writer and actor sometimes reduced to the role of raw materials for the expression of the director's vision.

This book will look at the ways in which good directors manage the whole process of getting a play from script to performance. It will look in detail at the relationship between directors and actors, how directors release creativity and optimize innovation, how they give space to the creative drives of performers but still maintain an outcome that is true to the original vision and delivered on time and within budget. It will also look at some of the craft skills of acting, as they relate to working within creative groups, and to some of the principles of creative working that seem to be universal across many artforms and how they may be applied outside the arts. But it will also examine the proposition that the arts, particularly the theater arts, do more than merely hold up a mirror to life. They reflect the fact that much of what we call "reality" is no more robust than the "illusions" of art. That how we are and how we behave in the real world is often a performance too.

The book divides roughly into three sections. The first four chapters look at the role of the director as a model for leadership in a creative context. The second section, Chapters 5 to 12, looks at creative teamwork and live communication. The final section, Chapters 13 to 15, is a collection of essays that explore the wider implications of applying artistic ideas and perceptions in the world.

CHAPTER 1

Creativity – Myths and Legends

A lot of myths surround creativity. Artists never really talk about it. They talk about "the work" and they talk about what they are doing, but they rarely talk about creativity in the abstract. There are, however, some basic general principles:

– *Nothing comes from nothing.* We are always starting from somewhere, the stuff in our heads, the existing marketplace; the history we all remember, the materials in front of us. There are no blank spaces in our heads and even the blank paper in front of us is a certain size and texture and absorbency that will limit what we can do with it. There are always initial conditions.

– *Metamorphosis is unstoppable.* All complex dynamic systems are spontaneously creative. If you leave a complex dynamic system alone and do nothing to it, it will change anyway. Leave your garden alone and it will gradually turn into a forest. Leave your car alone and it will gradually fall apart. Leave your people alone and they will come up with something.

– *Creativity is a boundary phenomenon.* Creativity happens on the edges of things, on the margins of an ecosystem, on the surface of a membrane, where a theory meets a fact, where a person meets their needs. Without boundaries to define it, there is no creative territory.

The creative process is fundamentally the same whether you are trying to write a new book or to develop a new theory of subatomic physics. Eventually you find yourself at the edge of what you have mastered; at the boundary of what comes easily, and yet your imagination has offered you a glimpse of another possibility. This other possibility will be rooted in what you know and what has been done elsewhere and it will be fragmentary: a misty vision, not clear, not complete. The gap between where you are and what is known, and what you can glimpse, in moments, in your imagination, becomes more and more difficult to endure. When this tension begins to be felt, you are usually heading in the right direction to be creative and original.

This uncomfortable place is where creative people spend a lot of their time, sometimes almost maddened by the difficulty of the problem before them and working at it obsessively to "break through" into the territory where things again begin to flow. Sometimes it is experienced as a kind of feverish excitement.

Many artists, particularly highly creative ones, spend most of their time there. Cézanne was famously agitated; Picasso refers to *"l'inquiétude"* of Cézanne – his essentially driven nature as he wrestled with the boundaries of what he wanted to do in painting. Murray Gell-Mann, the nuclear physicist who came up with the idea of quarks, describes the same thing; comparing experiences of the creative process among his fellow scientists, he observed:

> We had each found a contradiction between the established way of doing things and something we needed to accomplish: in art, the expression of a feeling, a thought, an insight; in theoretical science, the explanation of some experimental facts in the face of an accepted "paradigm" that did not permit such an explanation.

The creative juices get going when you are up against a boundary, at the edge of what is acceptable, possible, or known. And the thing that seems to drive people there are fragments of ideas, beliefs, visions, awkward facts, details that will not be ignored. People worry away at them until they drop through into another place where they at last make sense and can be expressed. Murray Gell-Mann describes this in terms of complexity mathematics, as finding a new "basin of attraction." This concept is a very useful one (Gell-Mann 1994).

There is a picture in James Gleick's book *Chaos* (Gleick 1987) that shows the solution of an equation, $x^4 - 1 = 0$, by Newton's method. This is a very complex equation (despite its apparent simplicity) and it has four possible answers that work. In Murray Gell-Mann's metaphor you could describe these answers as "basins of attraction," places where, however you begin to tackle the problem, you will end up with one of these four categories of solution. We can call them a red answer, a blue answer, a green answer and a yellow answer. But the interesting bit is the boundary between these possible solutions. It is, in this image, a fractal. Though it has a clear pattern (it looks a bit like a chain of swirling leaves) and although it is made of only four colors, the pattern is never exactly the same in two areas. It is, literally, infinitely complex.

When you are in the creative place you are in this infinitely complex territory. Things are not completely chaotic, with no discernable pattern, and they can look deceptively well-ordered at times, but they are contradictory, fluid. The right answer seems to change from moment to moment, so that a proposition that looked like a breakthrough suddenly has an obvious flaw. One is plagued by fragments of other solutions, none of them complete, none of them clearly right, or necessarily possible. One finds oneself stumbling about, thinking for a moment that the answer is all blue but then finding that there is a little green bit at the edge which simply does not belong there – that isn't right, that doesn't "work," as artists often say. This is the very early and most uncomfortable part of the creative process.

Great artists will be constantly pushing at the boundaries of what they know. They are always trying to inhabit this boundary territory, creating images that often, to others, are barbaric or insulting or nonsensical, constantly nagged by the fact that, although everyone does green paintings, or writes red books, they have imagined a kind of possibility of a sort of bluish one. They are constantly in pursuit of a different place, they are drawn towards (or are driven towards) this infinitely complex boundary zone. Sometimes they will succeed in expressing a transformational innovation and very often these innovators will be only the first, the earliest, to arrive in the new territory; territory which many others will have been struggling with and moving towards as well. Lonely geniuses are never lonely for long.

But even when they are in this muddled, semi-chaotic place they are still productive. They will be generating material, making attempt after attempt after attempt to capture what they have glimpsed, regardless of the uncertainty of a stable solution, carrying on even when there is no clear path or goal. Almost all of this production is never seen, even by the artist's close associates. It is burned or binned; a great deal of it is done unconsciously in restless, agitated reverie. Sometimes a stream of iterations is kept as a series of experiments, or preparatory sketches. Sometimes, after endless refining and exploration, an "answer" or at least some object is made that feels "finished" and the breakthrough can be presented to the world. It is as if these innovative solutions were already there, waiting to be discovered. They have been not so much created as found, enfolded, within the messy bits at the edges of what was already there – and of course potentially accessible to anyone with a similar mastery of the known field – they just needed to be dug out.

And it is this labor that often goes unseen or unnoticed by others. Some of it is done by the unconscious mind, and time needs to be allowed for that in the work. Lying-around-dozing time; going-to-the-pub time. Darwin used to walk round and round his garden "turning things over in his mind." Mozart and Shakespeare seem, interestingly, to be almost unique examples of artists who undertook this entire process in their minds. There is evidence that they did not write drafts, but were so skilful and of such capacious imagination, that they could do all this work in their heads and then write down the finished masterpiece uncorrected. Some artists and scientists report this ability for fragments, or short works, but lesser mortals work away at draft after draft after draft.

The persistence and singlemindedness that it takes to bash away at these barriers, to exist for prolonged periods within the infinitely complex boundary zone – and still keep working – marks the creative innovator from the average. Great artists, scientists or thinkers have a will to innovate, a will to make change happen. They are perhaps unusually tolerant of, or even addicted to, the restless anxiety of the creative space. And this is not a linear process. It cannot be simplified or laid out into a series of less difficult steps. It needs you to throw your whole self at it to work. And you need to begin before you can see the whole way ahead.

But in a much more modest way, this same process is with us all the time, in any situation we are in. We have the potential to find creative boundaries anywhere; we just need to put ourselves in the mindset of noticing them, because they are all around us. We are how we are, and we do what we do, mostly because it serves us fine and we have got into the habit. We do not often have the desire to make things different. Although we could …

CHAPTER 2

The Illusion of Leadership

Directing creativity

Directing a play is a creative process. At one level it is an exercise in efficient project management: there is the deadline of opening night, there are sets to be built, actors to be rehearsed and the whole thing must come together on time, on budget and be successful, or you go bust. However, to be successful the play must also innovate. Whatever it is, it must hit the audience as new, exciting, original and different, or they won't come. So theater people, particularly, have to innovate to stay in business. They also have to innovate within very tight constraints of timing and budget.

How do you get that balance between allowing for the creativity and innovation you need from all the people involved – designers, actors, technicians, marketing – while at the same time making sure you open on time, on budget?

The theater director as an artist is unusual, in that his material, his medium, is a group of people, rather than a collection of musical sounds or a range of pigments. The theater director cannot physically manipulate his materials to produce his results. His craft lies in manipulating the creative output of his cast and technicians to yield his results. He is close to an orchestral conductor, but perhaps could be said to have something more than an interpretive role. And unlike colors or sounds, people have ideas of their own and wills of their own.

Some of the director's constraints are like those of other artists: the shape of the performing area, the technical limitations of bodies and lights, and obviously the script. But the others are unique to the job of director and focus on the craft of directing the creativity of others. It is this aspect of the job that makes theater, of all the arts, particularly useful for bridging understanding between leaders of people in business and directors of people in an art form. Directing is about selection and interpretation. You are not just working with productions of your own hand or heart; you are collating and manipulating the productions of others. There is perhaps something fundamentally inauthentic in the director's role. Tyranny and despotism are ever present dangers, as is casual damage to the work and hearts of others. But all these dangers seem to me to be inherent in any managerial role.

Poets, fakes and sleeping lions

The theater director does not need to know much about how to act, or design a set, in order to have a positive effect on the work of other artists. Like a lion dozing by a waterhole when the other animals come down to drink, the mere presence of the director in the creative community is enough to galvanize it, if they conduct themselves in the right way. But one attribute the director does need is authority – power – or they will not be effective, and they need to embody it masterfully. This is sometimes easier to achieve than you might expect. The great director Peter Brook was once asked by a young student how to become a director in the theater and allegedly replied: "Tell everybody you are one and hope that they believe you." There is an important truth in this. The craft of leadership is one that is to do with how you are seen, as much as with how you are. It is about your physical presence and how you "handle" yourself and others. But the more important attribute of the director is to embody the balance between humility and power that authority requires: to be able to release and encourage the creative input and craftsmanship of the people involved in a production, and yet to maintain the authority that allows them, in the complex collaborative activity that is a play or film, to direct this creativity to an end that is beautiful and good and true.

Creativity lies in putting conjunctions in place; leadership consists in ensuring mastery of what is known, plus the attitude that balances the pursuit of mastery with the attitude of innovation. Reliable, enduring, successful innovation is always emergent from what is known. And the deeper the knowledge and the greater the mastery of what is known, the more robust, influential and enduring the innovation. One of the crucial factors in this is connected with the idea of authority and is at the heart of this model of creative leadership. It is to do with presence. In a rehearsal the director's presence, in every sense, is essential. This is about maintaining in the team the sense of what is expected of them. It is about charisma – but it is also a trick. It can be taught. Given the right signals, any group of people will project charisma onto their leader, regardless of what is actually going on inside the leader's head. This can be very useful, as it gives you, the director, time to think.

Creative leaders need to be able to identify, articulate and express constraints that provoke the team to creative responses within the right field. The constraints imply a direction, a hope for the investigation, but do not specify the means or, most importantly, the *specific* outcomes. They are also tight enough to constitute a strong challenge; they are not easy or clear paths. Necessity *is* the mother of invention: if we are not working against some resistance, if we are not up against some sort of boundary then we are not creative. But describing the nature of those boundaries in the right way allows us to control the direction of creative effort while allowing sufficient space for the unexpected or the superb to emerge.

It is clear from this that the details of language, expression and personal charisma are extremely important in creative leadership. Business pays little attention to the qualities of the language it uses, and a peculiar argot has evolved in the business community that makes the eloquence necessary for this kind of leadership very difficult (of which more later). Good creative leaders need to be able to speak like poets, with the same clarity and simplicity and passion.

But the obverse is also important: the use you make of silence and of listening – of what you do NOT say. The best directors say very little. They balance their interventions with silence, but they stay in the room and they watch what happens and they listen. They are constantly looking out for the fragment of an idea that might lead to an innovation. They are vigilant; they maintain the creative gaze.

The gaze

There is something extremely powerful about being observed at work. When actors are rehearsing there is a profound difference in the work they do when the director is in the room and the work they do when they are not. Even when as an assistant director you are present and working well with the company, there is a qualitative difference in how they work when the director is there. People seem to be acutely conscious of who really matters, in the sense of who is holding the narrative that will make sense of their work.

This is, I think, more than merely an issue of rank or status. In the theater, the director is not the boss in the sense of the employer. As an actor one does not associate the director with the one who may hire you or fire you, or may reward you in financial terms. The director is the one who is making sense of what you do. They are the only one who, as an actor, you can finally trust to help you make sense of what you are doing and give you the encouragement and the coaching that will allow you to be better. Your fellow actors may have views but they cannot judge the impact of your actions on the audience, nor are they responsible for it. There is a custom in the theater that actors generally refrain from giving advice to one another: that is the director's job.

At a fairly basic level what you want is the director's attention. You want them to see what you are doing so they can help and guide. There is a strong parent–child element to the relationship. But for some reason, in my experience of the theater, it was almost always benign. If you had no respect for the director and did not trust their judgment it could be very difficult and often produced acute anxiety among the actors, but if there was at least a modicum of respect for them then their presence was always a boost to your efforts.

In organizations I have rarely seen this emphasis on the presence of the boss or manager in the room being acknowledged for its real power. It always seems to me that leaders and managers in organizations other than the theater have another job besides directing that they have to do, as well as directing their ensemble. So in fact they are very rarely present; and, when they are, they are not present with the sense of disinterested scrutiny that is the hallmark of the director in a rehearsal. And of course there is profound fear in today's workplaces of the parental implications of the kind of relationship I am advocating. Everything about present work relations is in flight from the potentially patronizing, authoritarian or hierarchical. Even actual parents are in flight from these relations.

In most organizations, people's experience of their line managers is that they briefly appear, listen a bit, give a few instructions and then go away again to do whatever they do. Most people therefore are essentially working on their own, without a presence to coach and guide them as they work. The management's presence is felt only as a carrot or a stick. Their presence lingers as a target or a goal or a deadline, rarely as an eloquent suggestion, or a personal inspiration, or a trusted guide.

Creative constraints and how to use them

Theater directors have a skill in framing constraints for others in a way that will provoke them to excited creative activity and produce work that is aligned with the director's vision for the final piece. In business I see managers who are very much in the role of theater directors and yet are not only unable to frame problems in this way but also often in the position of actively inhibiting the creative potential of staff by offering only *restraints* – external targets and prohibitions rather than active choices – that have the effect of holding people back from creative responses. This means that most managers spend a lot of time in a state that an artist would recognize as being "blocked" – turning over ideas and possibilities entirely in the abstract, unable to see that to begin wrong is better than not to begin at all.

Creative leadership is a balancing act between the emergent and the directed: the implicit evolutionary changes that will happen in spite of, or without, your interventions and the desired changes that can be encouraged by your actions and directions.

Look at these statements: They are all giving directions but with a different degree of constraint involved:

- "Go left now."

- "Tend towards the left."

- "What if you look over there?"

Each of these represents a different place on a scale of autonomy for the person being directed. These three statements also have a time dimension. The first expects an immediate response with a known outcome, the second provides a general rule to be used often, with perhaps unforeseen consequences, and the third might involve hunting around for days, but might turn up something really interesting.

As a general rule, encouraging autonomy and creativity will gain you commitment and enthusiasm but lose you control of the detail. Gaining control of the detail will generally loose you commitment and enthusiasm. With a well-crafted constraint you can get both.

Using constraints as interventions and then letting them run permits you to continuously adjust the degree of autonomy and therefore of creative emergence that you allow in the mix. And it is the degree of creative autonomy that is strongly linked to the commitment and enthusiasm of the team.

If you say to a group of people, "Here are some bits and pieces of rope and sticks and canvas. I want you to improvise a scene using them," they may come up with something exciting, they will find it hard, and they may or may not have a stimulating adventure.

If you give the same materials and say, "Here are some bits and pieces of rope and some canvas. I want you to use these things and your own bodies and voices to make an elephant that dances," they will be more likely to have a stimulating experience and come up with something remarkable. They will certainly attack the problem more quickly and with more energy. But they will be working within a narrower field. The irony is that increasing the constraints, liberates creative energy.

Read these sets of instructions slowly and carefully and imagine how you would respond:

- "Here is some paper and a whole range of colored paint and a brush. Paint me a picture of a rainbow." What would you do?

- "Here is some black ink and some paper. Use them somehow to make an image of a rainbow." What would you do?

- "Go into the woods and collect some stuff to bring back here and make it into a picture of a rainbow." What would you do?

The objective is the same in each. The people know exactly what a rainbow is accepted to be. The constraints are varied to provoke them into re-examining the proposition "rainbow" and figuring out other paths to expressing it; each iteration provides new ideas about how the fundamental proposition might be expressed.

The same could be said of examining the proposition "Hamlet" or "Beyond Petroleum." The director setting up the constraints does not know what the group will come up with. They are providing the director with the material with which to crystallize their vision.

There are always initial conditions and there must always be an understanding of "what play we are in," some common understanding of the proposition to be explored. The director's vision for the final outcome does not need to be complete, indeed it must not be, but the director must be able to get across a set of initial conditions that are held in common. In the case above he or she must ensure that everyone knows we are looking for a new way of making rainbows. In the case of the theater, that is usually clear and written down; it is the script everyone is working on. "We are doing *Hamlet*, we know the story (roughly) – we are not doing *Macbeth*."

Once the proposition to be explored has been articulated and the process begun, the director must then be present and must be vigilant. Metamorphosis is unstoppable; once people start to respond to the constraints and start to create, they will diverge. There must be a selecting eye, a vigilant gaze, watching the efforts of the group to be able to select and encourage the iterations that are going roughly in the right direction, and to lead them away from dead-ends. The way to do that is to set a new challenge, redefine the constraints; so that if the group's efforts seem to be going in an unprofitable direction, they can be encouraged forward into a new challenge. The dead-end is fine; it will have taught the group something. There is no need to dwell on it. When making art there are no mistakes, there are just things that don't work.

Creativity is a boundary phenomenon; it will occur where resistance is encountered, where things collide, where the awkward or unexpected or hilarious appears. It is the director's job to ensure that these encounters happen by setting challenging and imaginative constraints. It is also the director's job to ensure that the group and the wider organization are equipped to cope with them when they occur. Group creative work requires high levels of trust and privacy and a sense of equality before the task. Status games and hierarchy are antithetical to creativity in groups.

The leadership illusion

Regardless of the projections and emotions that the director–ensemble relationship generates there is nothing particularly special about leaders. They are the ones that look and they are the ones that choose. Anyone can do it. There are no special qualities required. Leadership, in this context, is an illusion. Leaders have no particular map or insight or personal quality that marks them as radically different from anyone else in the troupe. The troupe colludes in accepting the leader's assertion that they can lead. And they will have an effect, even if they turn out to be unskilled in the role. If they are unskilled they will not last long. But it is a matter of skill, that is all – a mask that can be handed to anyone for a time. What matters in leading for creativity is what you say and how you say it, how you handle yourself with the group, how you perform the role – the details of your moment-to-moment interactions with the group. Like any work of art, the illusion is created by the practical skill with which the artist handles his or her medium of expression. In the case of the director, that medium is your physical self and other people and their ideas.

The characteristics of the theater director that I have outlined above seem to me to define a style of leadership that is rare outside the arts. For lots of good political and social reasons the behaviors and relationships implicit in this leadership style have been organized out of the workplace. The dominance of the science and engineering paradigm has become deeply embedded in workplace culture and it is pretty effective. If you want consistency, and as long as the work done by an organization is in some sense mechanical, then engineering thinking is fine. It is appropriate to talk of silos and matrices and inputs and outputs. It is also, perhaps, appropriate to manage by numbers, targets, goals and quotas.

But increasingly in the West, and for large sectors of the global economy, we are no longer doing work that has anything to do with engineering. We are not making money from manufactures. We are generating wealth by making relationships, doing deals, advising; by delivering experiences, visions, pleasures, reassurance. We are creating ideas and giving performances. Such activities require a different kind of organization, and different styles of management and leadership. If we are truly to benefit from the cultural wealth of our society and use it to secure our place in the world economy now that manufacturing has, to all intents and purposes, gone elsewhere, we need to seriously rethink how we train and develop our leaders and managers.

But there is another imperative. The degree of complexity and connectedness in society is increasing exponentially. We seem to be entering a highly volatile and essentially unknowable future. Five-year planning is impossible (if it ever was possible). We are beginning to understand that the future is indeed unpredictable. There is therefore a high premium on the ability to behave flexibly and responsively to the present. We need to be nimble, adaptable and inventive to survive. All these qualities are there in the arts. Artists have been living to these specifications for generations. It is not a particularly pleasant way to live. There are many aspects of the creative life that are deeply uncomfortable, but the methods and organizational structures that allow for all of the above are available to us. However, they require us to behave very differently in the way we lead and organize.

When we are working in groups someone needs to be in charge. But they need to be in charge with an understanding that they are not therefore also in control. Power in all social animals is mobile. It is handed around the troupe depending on what is to be done; on whether the task in hand is sex or defense or food or fun. Who has the power is communicated by actions, gestures and sounds. At work we are engaged in tasks where, on the face of it, food, defense, sex or fun are not what we are doing, so anyone can lead us, although of course, being human, we often get muddled about what we are doing and all these aspects of our behavior have a habit of intruding among us whatever we are doing. The group they are in charge of can only be of a certain size – small enough to have the intimacy of connections that will allow for trust and creativity to emerge (about twenty-five people is about right). But the director's role is just that, a role, like a parent's. Anyone can be one, some are better at it than others, but anyone can be taught to do it well. It's just a matter of how you behave.

Directing vs. managing – the Russian experiment

The following is an exercise I did with a group of Russian students in a desperate attempt to communicate the fundamental difference of approach that I believe lies behind the managerial/engineering approach to leadership and the directorial/creative approach. Like a good rehearsal, this exercise was dreamed up in the moment, in the middle of a workshop. I hadn't really planned it, and it was thrown together on the spur of the moment: I was working with a mixed group of about twenty MBA students.

At the other end of the large room in which we were working there were a lot of chairs dotted about. I divided the students into two groups.

I then chose someone to lead one of the groups and I gave the group a rough hierarchy. I grabbed a student and told her "You are the boss." I grabbed another and said "You are second in command, and the others must obey your orders." I then told the group boss what the task was: "I want you to organize these people to get those chairs over there down to this end of the room as quickly as possible – Go!"

There was a little delay as the team made an attempt to organize themselves. The boss gave a few instructions to the second-in-command but some of the group were already drifting off towards the chairs so the boss just said "OK. Get the chairs!" The group moved fairly quickly up the room; they neatly stacked the chairs. The boss hovered about a bit giving a bit of encouragement and the group carried back the stacks of chairs.

I asked them to reflect a bit on what that was like while I turned to the other team and addressed them as if I was directing a scene in a play: "I want you to imagine we are all at a very grand garden party. We are inside, sipping champagne and outside those chairs over there are covered in beautiful silk damask." (I paused for a few seconds; some of them half-mimed sipping champagne.) "Suddenly there is a clap of thunder and it starts to pour with rain and we all rush out to get the chairs in before they are ruined OK? CRASH! THUNDER!"

They shriek with delight and rush at the chairs in a frenzy and grab them. They rush down the room and the chairs are dumped in a heap at the other end of the room and everyone is rushing about so much that one girl never gets to carry a chair. The task is completed marginally quicker than the other group.

So what?

As the two groups began to talk and reflect, they offered fragments of their experience of the game and their observations; some interesting and fundamental principles began to emerge:

- "The leader team was slower and neater."

- "It was a boring task."

- "There was too much bossing."

- "It was slow, regimented and dull."

- "The other team was chaotic but fast."

- "It was really fun."

- "I want to do it again!"

Then we began to discuss an interesting question: "If you are to get better at this the next time – what do you do?" It was generally agreed that, probably, the first team will improve what it already does; incrementally improving the method of stacking, the order of collection, the who does what, getting faster and more efficient at the first solution that the group evolved from its own tacit knowledge and expectations of the task and of life in a hierarchy. The second team, however, was presented with a host of questions about the nature of the task to be considered before the next attempt:

–   "Does it matter if the chairs are dumped in a heap as long as we get them in really quick?"

–   "Do we need all the people we have – as one girl was redundant?"

From my point of view, as leader of that team, I was delighted by their commitment to the task, and completely surprised by the fact that they just dumped the chairs in a heap. I had never expected that. And there was a fundamental difference of attitude between the groups. The first group were expecting to wait to be told what to do next and all the second group were keen to try again and to offer ideas for improving or radically changing the performance.

There is something fundamental here – the magic "What if … ?" Playing out the vision of the task, and letting the actors self-organize, reaches a category of solution totally different from the solution suggested by the hierarchy model. The imagination team are in a place to explore different possibilities and approaches to the chair-collecting problem, and will not only come up with different ways of doing it very easily, but also, *by* doing it in these ways, will invite deeper reflection on the real nature of the problem. This seems to me to be a key difference between the creative style and the managerial style of leadership. Creative leadership thinks as it works. But with the managerial or hierarchical style, any change of practice will require you to stop and go elsewhere to think – redesign your process and come back: novelty is less likely to emerge from the process of doing and when it does, it is more likely to be seen as a problem than as an opportunity.

One of the fundamentals of the creative style is that you have a leader who can frame the task so that the led will be delighted to attack it and bring their imaginations with them as they do: so that in the doing there is divergence and serendipity, and the leader is present to observe this unexpected material and use it to select the constraints with which to frame the next attempt at the task. It will also mean, of course, that you cannot define in detail the outcome. In organizations, I often see people trained to go straight to outcomes: "Get to the goal as fast and as efficiently as possible." What this imprecation leaves out, is the time and space to discover if this is the best goal.

Goals and targets and all the other language of objectives have the unambiguous simplicity of sport; as if complex tasks were like football games where all the rules are known and all the rules are obeyed. Goals and targets bring with them all the assumptions that the first group in the exercise described above experienced. They allow management without connection. They substitute for the parent/child relationship. They relieve managers of their duty of care to their team and deny managers the possibility of being delighted and surprised by what their people can come up with.

But of course goals and targets can also act as creative constraints, albeit poorly framed ones. A kind of negative version of creative emergence comes into play, as we shall see later. Depending how leaders on the ground frame the goals, there is plenty of room for creative emergence. But without a director – vigilant, engaged, present, like a good parent – what is emerging may go off in a direction of its own. People may find ways of achieving the numbers by routes that will, in the medium or longer term, destroy as much value as they create.

Why setting targets is a waste of time

Targets are the same as constraints, except that they are not expressed in a way that makes them any use for creative leadership. Targets, like constraints, will always stimulate creativity but they are usually expressed as numbers, not with well-chosen words. Economists call creativity "gaming" (or cheating), which roughly means achieving the numerical target in some lateral, imaginative way that the guy who set the target didn't think of.

Given targets and incentives, people will cheat (be creative) about how they achieve them. This is not really "cheating", this is the wonderful force of the artistic imagination – "cheating" is an example of creative emergence. It is the creative imagination in action. We should be managing and leading this, not trying to prevent or eliminate it. Watching and learning from the inventiveness of cheats allows us to innovate. The dance of innovation and counter-measure that is currently going on between internet fraudsters and spammers, and those who have other aims for the internet, is a truly emergent, creative place. We need both to exist for creative emergence to happen.

Targets make it possible to produce the measurable changes that economists need to tick their boxes, but in complex, emergent systems the creative response to the constraint of a target can skew the whole thing so that the damage caused by unforeseen consequences can undermine or destroy the value added by achieving the numbers. Numerical targets work like any other creative constraint: they stimulate creativity in the journey to fulfil them, but they give you no control over the interesting material that emerges on the way. You end up at the right target but maybe by the wrong path.

A good example of this is the target the British government set to reduce the amount of time people had to wait in Accident and Emergency (A&E) before being seen by a medic. They set a target that "No one should wait in A&E more than four hours before being admitted to a ward, transferred or discharged." This unleashed a torrent of creative responses:

–   Massaging the figures with a series of clever statistical lies that meant it looked like no one was waiting more than four hours.

–   Holding patients outside in the ambulance until they were ready to process them. If they were still in the ambulance, maybe they would be regarded as "not waiting in A&E."

–   Getting in a load of gurneys, taking the wheels off, calling them "beds" and making people lie on them in a corridor and calling it "the pre-admission ward."

–   Some hospitals even cancelled scheduled operations on other patients to release funds for hiring extra doctors for A&E.

These are all what I call creative responses. In each of them, although they are "cheats" in one sense, there is the possible germ of a good idea. Each cheating strategy, each creative iteration, generates ideas that could be developed into parts of a good solution. Managing by numbers, instead of by art, misses all the creative possibilities the workforce is exploring for you.

These unexpected responses to the imposition of the targets each suggest further creative possibilities you could explore:

–   What if we look in more detail at the way waiting list statistics are compiled?

–   What if mobile treatment centers could be used for some cases, and patients sent home directly from the mobile unit?

–   What if we could design really good, safe and effective mobile beds?

–   What if some classes of medical care were provided outside the NHS altogether?

The problem with targets is the way they are expressed. They deliver the numbers the bean-counters like to have, but they also generate unforeseen consequences and creative responses that deliver the numbers, but not the intention behind the numbers. These unforeseen consequences get labeled as "cheating" when in fact they are the raw material of innovation. The problem is that the there is no one there to observe and encourage them, so they are dismissed as problems rather than welcomed as interesting possibilities.

The uncarved block

An example of a good constraint, a proper creative one, not a target, is the legend that goes with the development of the Sony Walkman.

The story goes like this:

The CEO goes down to the research labs where all the eggheads are working. He gathers them round and he pulls out of his shirt pocket a small block of wood. He holds it up and he says: "Make me a tape-player this big." He puts it down on the table and he leaves.

This is a good constraint. It is concrete and specific. The guys can pick it up and start measuring. They can respond immediately and the challenge focuses them immediately in the right direction.

But this is really such a good constraint because of what was NOT said:

—   He did not say "Make me the smallest tape-recorder you can." (They'd still be at it.)

—   He did not say "Make me a small portable tape player." (They might come up with something just too big to fit in your shirt pocket.)

—   He did not say "Make something new and revolutionary that will let people play music wherever they want." (No point in encouraging them to reinvent the wheel.)

—   He did not email them a set of specifications. (How would they tell he cared about the outcome?)

He went in there in person; he gave a controlled and gnomic performance in front of the people who would be doing the work. He left plenty of space for them to imagine, invent and innovate but within concrete and specific boundaries that he had personally communicated. He had a partial vision of the desired outcome, but he had no idea how it would finally turn out.

He did not give them a target to hit; he gave them a field to play in.

CHAPTER 3

Project-Managing a Work of Art

You can look at the process of getting a play on stage as a simple series of steps in the creative pathway:

- The writer writes a play.

- The director and the designer agree on a design for the set and costumes.

- The director works with the ensemble of actors to rehearse the play.

- The actors perform the play for the audience.

First, usually, someone writes a play, or, much less often, a play is devised or co-written by the ensemble. Whichever process is used, there is always, at some stage, a script. A script is a long way from a performance, but it contains a lot of stuff. All that is said in the final event is written there, plus sometimes some character descriptions or guide lines about locations and prompts about how things should be performed. In a conventional process it is usually a director who will read and reflect on a play and decide to mount a production. The roles of the producers, who may fund and promote the production, do not concern us here.

The next part in the creative process is to engage a designer. The designer's role is key in a large production and very often, in a large production, decisions about the design will have to be made long before the actors start rehearsing. The creative input of the designer shapes the world in which the play will unfold.

The next step is to engage the actors and begin rehearsals. In terms of time spent on getting the production together, the rehearsals are often the shortest part of the process; finding producers or raising funding may take much longer in some cases. Directors often mull their ideas for a production for many years and conversations with designers may go on for weeks or months before rehearsal commences. Of course time spent "working" in a creative way is not measured as it is in other fields. Thinking, mulling and pondering are all part of the creative process. Ideas will gestate for many years in the unconscious. The time involved should not be measured merely in the hours of face-to-face contact with people.

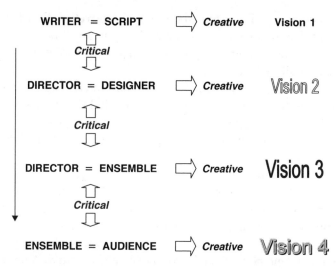

Figure 3.1 How to get a play from the page to the stage.

After the rehearsals the production is brought to the stage and then presented to the audience. The interaction with the audience is also a creative process, a vital one and one over which the director has of course no control. The day-to-day performance also requires creative input of a subtle kind from the performers. But generally at this stage the director will leave the production, his or her work done. And apart from the occasional visit to ensure the production has not moved and developed too far from the form arrived at in rehearsal, the director's creative input is over. Sometimes the production will be handed over to an assistant director to maintain standards in performance and coach understudies. You could depict the process crudely as is done in Figure 3.1.

I have given the diagram two axes. Across the diagram, you could describe the relationships and activities as being fundamentally creative. At each stage in the process, looking across the diagram, you are looking for the most imaginative and innovative solutions you can find; you are on an open-ended creative journey and everyone needs to think like an artist. Communication needs to be non-hierarchical and co-creational.

I have characterized the process moving down the diagram as essentially critical, not only in the sense of a critical path in project management, but also in the sense that you are obliged to police these levels quite strictly. You need to be the law-giver and judge.

If you are the director of the project you are of course responsible for delivering it on time and on budget. It is your responsibility to minimize the modifications forced on you or adapt them to keep the project moving forward successfully. There must be minimal innovation *between* the levels, or the project will begin to fall apart. But you need maximum innovation *within* each level to ensure you get an innovative solution and the full engagement of all involved.

If the actors start to come up with too many interesting suggestions to alter the design, for instance, the process may grind to a halt. Similarly, the designer should not suggest modifications to the script to accommodate their design ideas. Creativity and emergence up and down the diagram can be a disaster.

However, within the field defined by each level you want to maximize creative responses. For example, you might, after long exploration and deliberation, working with the designer, arrive at the idea of performing *Hamlet* entirely in the nude, with actors wearing only feather boas. Then your job is to offer these constraints to the actors in such a way that they will accept them and be provoked into a creative response to them. How can the actors get going on the challenge of *Hamlet* in the nude? How will they do the fights? What will happen in the intimate bedroom scenes? How will you murder Polonius with only a feather boa? How will you distribute the parts and make it clear to the audience who is who? How can the Boas be used to suggest different ranks of society? The creative process thrives on constraint. It would be barmy and very difficult to do a production like this, but given an attitude that accepts the constraints with enthusiasm, solutions to the seemingly impossible challenge of the task might begin to emerge.

Having some constraints makes you more creative, not less. This understanding and acceptance of constraints is a core value in making theater. Where it becomes eroded, problems can occur. One of the director's most important functions is to present the constraints as exciting challenges and to give enough context for the actors to be able to begin their creative process and become involved and enthusiastic about the challenge. At other times the director will need to police the constraints. As the exploration proceeds and new possibilities emerge, the director must have the ability to prevent the demands for trousers undermining the courage of the performers, ruining the budget and throwing out the costume department's schedule. Most of this comes down to the deft use of status and communication skills (of which much more later).

This leads us to the core concept in creative leadership. Decisions made at each level define the boundaries, and provide the constraints within which the creative endeavors of the next group must operate.

There is still a good discipline in the theater about this, which is central to the creative process in theater. Improvisation, one of the principal creative tools for actors, depends on the idea of accepting constraints. Improvisation proceeds, and creativity is unleashed, by the discipline of saying "yes" to whatever is offered and working with that. This principle is at the heart of creative work in groups. As a director or leader of this creative process, however, you need to both stimulate the creative response of people at each stage and at the same time be ready to define and police the constraints between them. While it is true that this accepting attitude to constraints, this readiness to view the givens as the material from which ideas come, is common to all artists in whatever field, it seems also to be rare in business.

The (misty) vision thing

In many organizations there is often a desire for more stuff to resolve problems with. Extra resources will fix it. There are many reasons for this. Some are to do with status games and empire-building and so on, but there is also the reluctance to bring to bear that attitude of creative making do. It smacks of a lack of ambition. In many cases more resources is a fine idea, but if resources are abundant and there are no constraints then there is usually a climate of waste and often of de-motivating complacency. In art this is often described as being stuck. A fat advance, a heap of clean paper, a state-of-the-art word processor and a stretch of uninterrupted time to work more often than not produce paralysis and depression rather than a new book.

In making theater, however, the constraints are not chosen by the director alone. At each stage in the theater-making process the creative contribution of others is not only encouraged but essential. Only the actors can solve the problems of performance and delivery; only the designer can get the colors right. At every stage the good director is encouraging in these creative inputs. The result of this is that the vision modifies as it goes. The core may remain the same and it is the director's job to keep it so, but for a truly successful and innovative (and happy) process it is essential for the vision and ideas of others to be allowed to appear and shape the final end.

This is the hardest part – but it is also accepted in the theater that this evolutionary process will take place. Artists do not expect to know in detail what the final event will be like. Indeed that is one of the exciting elements of making art – the sense of journeying into the unknown, of not being at all sure how things will finally turn out. In extreme cases, when the journey has been a long and difficult one, someone on the way may want to take their name off the credits when they see the final result, but this is not common. They may not agree with the final interpretation but they will usually accept it as a valid idea.

The final stage of this page-to-stage process is to place the finished work in front of the audience. Theater audiences these days are comparatively passive. They sit in silence in the dark, maybe laughing, maybe nodding off, and then they either tell their friends it was good and you have a hit, or they don't and you move on to the next job. But the audience's responses are also profoundly creative. They make the final meaning of the piece. This is true of all art; it is only in the moment of contact between the artwork and the audience that the thing comes to life, has meaning and power. And this is a profoundly creative act, particularly in the theater, where the audience has to do a lot of work to accept the painted faces and painted walls as representing some kind of version of their lives.

But this phenomenon is just as true in business. What the consumers finally make of your offer is often a surprise. In the telecoms industry the mobile phone and the internet are daily being worked on by the public as they playfully explore the possibilities of the technology and make new discoveries about what it could be for. The success of texting took the industry completely by surprise. The fashion for downloading is transforming the music industry. These innovations are led by the creativity of the audience, not the industry. There are many examples of this process in business but few organizations really seem to have grasped the opportunity it represents. The whole process of creativity and innovation is, increasingly often, falling outside the locus of influence of organizations.

When people do respond in this way to an organization's products, who then within the organization can take on the role of director and observe the creative work being done by consumers and direct it towards appropriate ends? If part of the creative ensemble is outside the organization and the work of innovation is being done there, who is directing this production? To what extent are they responsible for the experiments when they are a success, or if they are negative or dangerous? Who gets the rewards of successful innovations and who takes the rap for dangerous ones?

The perfect audience of one

What good theater directors do is observe, with intense concentration, in order to know truly what is going on in the scene before them. They observe, reflect, pinpoint what the actor is doing wrong, then use that insight to frame a constraint in the form of a positive challenge that *may* lead the actor in the right direction (or at least roughly in the direction that the director wants). They then do feedback. But the best feedback is precise, carefully selected detail. It's not just about being positive, it's about being positive and being useful, by framing a challenge for the person being managed that will liberate them into an effort that might yield the result you are looking for (although it might yield something different).

It requires presence, authority, vigilance and the ability to describe constraints as exciting challenges – to ask the right questions.

There is no benefit or usefulness to be had from feeding back to the actor a description of their error. It discourages them and it wastes time. The fact that they were too slow or too gentle with what they did in that iteration is irrelevant. There is an assumption (almost always justified) that they were not being too slow in order to deliberately mess up the rehearsal. They were being too slow because they were trying something out. Or they thought that was the best way.

For the director to say "That's much too slow. Do it again" will only get a discouraged actor, an unthinking increase in speed and a lack of engagement of the actor with their own performance, and perhaps the beginning of a resentment of the directors interventions in general. Notes are always given positively. Whatever the iteration, however appalling, good directors operate on the assumption that the actor is making an effort and that the effort needs to be acknowledged. Every offer is therefore greeted with encouragement: "Thank you, that's great … " even though the director might have been sitting there thinking "Oh my God, this is glacial, he's completely missed the moment. The audience will die of boredom if he does it like that … "

None of this is of use to the actor. The director needs to reflect on exactly what the actor is doing that is producing the effect. Is it the pace of speech? Are they too physically relaxed? Have they misread or misinterpreted a line? Have they missed something further back in the scene that leads to this?

Having developed a theory about why, the director then needs to frame a constraint that might liberate the actor into the required behavior. Perhaps by going back and doing the speech again, but this time imagining they are twenty minutes late for a meeting, or that it is pouring with rain outside, or that they are very angry. Only then does the director open their mouth and offer the suggestion to the actor.

What the actor receives is encouragement and an exciting challenge: "OK, that's great, very good. Can you go back to the beginning of the scene and let's just try it as if you're really late and pissed off with yourself; OK? Just give it a go." This might yield the speed you need and, if it does not, another attempt may be necessary. It also, of course, might yield something else altogether. It might provoke an idea in the actor. It might illuminate something in the scene that the director had not noticed. It might even yield something that allowed the director to see that the actor was right about being slow. The job of the director is to watch. To notice what is going on and to reflect it back to the actors. The director is the perfect audience of one.

In the early stages of rehearsal, when everyone in the room is trying to create something, it is essential to maintain an atmosphere of total encouragement and acceptance, and to offer opportunity after opportunity to try different solutions to the problems of the scene. The director's task is to coax and nudge this work in the direction they want. Later, when the ideas are set and the fundamental decisions have been made, more direct and straightforward notes can be given.

It is manipulative. But it is positive and it keeps everyone in a place where they are secure and confident enough to attack the director's suggestions with passion and commitment and of course to offer suggestions and ideas of their own.

I rarely see this dynamic in place in other situations. There is often, in organizations I visit, a strong culture of feedback and plain speaking. This is all well and good, but if there is not with it a profound sense of trust and mutuality, it can be wholly negative and will always inhibit rather than encourage creative risk-taking and daring. People in organizations where there is a plain-speaking culture quickly develop a brittle carapace and normalize their behaviors around the implicit hierarchy. They reduce their possibility for creativity and surprise.

This is basic coaching technique, but is seldom in place in informal groups. It also puts a much greater emphasis on observation and reflection in the role of the leader than I usually see. There is something energizing and exciting about being observed at work in this way, by someone who is not judging you or looking for errors but is only going to offer you encouragement and challenge. There is no need, in these circumstances for any other kind of feedback. There is some evidence that this entirely positive frame is common to all successful creative groups. The level of trust that exists between the group and the leader and the mutual faith that everyone is making their best endeavors removes the need for negative feedback altogether (Whatmore 1999).

Summary

In Figure 3.1, at every stage along the way it is the director's job to maximize creativity *across* the diagram, but to minimize and contain it *down* the diagram (in order to stay on budget and on schedule). Once the costumes have been designed they cannot be redesigned by the actors. Once the play is rehearsed the words cannot be changed in performance.

To make the vision original and innovative, the director needs to encourage creative conversations, using openness and empathy at each stage across the diagram. To maintain the project on time and on budget, the director needs to use the aspects of the vision established so far to provide the creative constraints with which to direct the next level down the diagram. (I have called this "critical" in the dual sense of a "critical path" and in contrast to the creative styles of communication across the diagram.) The aspects of the project decided at each level then form the boundaries within which creative exploration is encouraged at the next level. It is the director's job to describe these givens in the form of inspiring challenges to which the team can be encouraged to respond creatively.

At each stage of evolution of the project, the initial vision will change and be modified by the creative input of all the people involved. The final vision that emerges will be different, sometimes radically different, from the writer's first vision. The leaders of the project must have the humility to accept this if they are to allow for the possibility of real innovation and if they are to maintain the commitment of all involved.

And finally the audience make their creative contribution, completing the process and hopefully responding with passion and commitment to the product you have made.

In managing this process, the director needs to be flexible in their approach. They must be able to illicit the behaviors that will encourage ideas at one phase and then be able to police the constraints that these ideas imply at the next. They must be constantly vigilant for the surprising and the unexpected, and have the authority to select and explore it when it occurs. The vital sets of skills are communication skills: use of language, of status play, of personality and of presence.

CHAPTER 4

Great Directing: A Case Study

The two most inspiring directors I worked with had one thing in common – an intensity of concentration. They neither of them said much but they possessed a powerful aura of focused concentration. For an actor, it was this sense of being rigorously observed that made them so stimulating to work for. You felt that they were not necessarily judging or even supporting you. Their gaze was dispassionate and you believed that behind it was an intense intellect studying what you did and vigilant for genius.

They would not fail to notice when you succeeded in something and you had a sense that they were merely indifferent to your failures. They expected failure and were not bothered by it. They were not going to blame you or be depressed by your lack of success. They were just going to sit there and watch intently for sparks of life to be encouraged. They were the perfect audience of one. They were giving you their complete, undivided attention.

There was an expectation implicit in the behavior of these directors: they were looking for something rare, which they knew it might not be easy to find. It was not that they had the answers, but you trusted that they were after something very special from you, even if neither you, nor they, could describe exactly what it was. And you also believed that by virtue of having given you the job, *they* believed you had a good chance of finding it.

When they spotted it, they supported and encouraged. When you were searching they let you wander about, but when you were stuck, no longer flowing with ideas, they would assist, either with specific technical input or with creative challenges – "What if ... ?" questions:

- "What if you are trying to get her to kiss you when you say it?"

- "What if we imagine this scene is outside, and you can't hear each other for the noise of the rain?"

- "What if the servants are trying to overhear what you say?"

Some of these suggestions you knew might have been close to the director's desire for the final interpretation of the scene, but you always had a sense that they were given in the spirit of provisional offerings to be explored, rather than instructions for how to do the scene. Constraints of any sort will always stimulate creativity: people will be obliged to explore and use different physical and emotional tools to pursue their objectives, and this will inevitably broaden the range of interpretations so that discoveries will be made.

The idea of constraining people of course implies power over them, authority. The best directors have a towering position in the hierarchy but don't play status in the rehearsal room. They are often disarmingly low-status – admitting doubt, seeking, honest about mistakes or reversals. They have a strong vision of their own but it is misty, incomplete. They weave the final vision from the ideas of the people in the room, clarifying it as they go, and they do that by using creative constraints. But when they see an innovation they have the authority to name it and fix it in the production.

In order to illustrate some of these ideas I will take a detailed look at the work of one director. This account is a conflation of experiences; it is subjective and it is a memoir. It is not a bit of research. It is a description of getting a play from page to stage which produced a dramatically successful outcome (the play and the director won several awards), although it was a very low-budget production. And it launched the career of the director and a number of the actors involved.

Rehearsing *King Lear*

The play was *King Lear* and it was I think the third or fourth production that that group had attempted. We began in a scruffy rehearsal room in North London. The director had from the start a particular charisma. She was tall and reserved but also easily amused. She laughed readily and seemed strong. We began the process not by reading the play but by engaging in many days of ensemble games and exercises. Before we even looked at the play we worked together playing trust and concentration games some of which are outlined in this book.

Eventually we began work on the text. This was done by everyone sitting round a large table and transliterating the play into modern English. But there was an interesting constraint. We were not allowed to interpret what we thought a line "really meant;" we had to find a contemporary form of words that simply clarified or updated what was written in the old Elizabethan text.

If the line was "What is your will, my lord?" we could transliterate that as "What would you like me to do, sir?" but any interpretation such as "He's trying to ingratiate himself with his master" was forbidden. This was an unusual constraint for an actor. Much acting training invites and encourages actors to explore "motivation," finding the intention behind the words. As I later found out, this was not an idea that was around in the Elizabethan age.

When we had done this painstaking work, over several days, with games and exercises in the morning and text work in the afternoons, we were allowed to read the lines of the play we were to perform. In this case one of the constraints the director put in place was that the text was to be performed uncut (an unusual choice for a play as long and "difficult" as *King Lear*).

But when we did the reading, there was another constraint. We were not allowed to read our own roles. We read the play several times and each time the casting was changed so that after the third or fourth reading of the whole piece we had read the play from the point of view of all the characters with whom we had most interaction or affinity. Regan, Goneril and Cordelia all read their sisters' roles, Kent and Gloucester and Lear all read each other's roles and as many of the other characters as possible were able to get a feel for the journey of their principle antagonists. Only after all this work was done did we read the whole text through, each hearing for the first time ourselves and others inhabit the roles were would play in the end.

The effect of this rigorous and painstaking process was very profound. Not only had we all been obliged to study in detail the whole of the story; we all had a feel of the objective narrative. It was in a sense the opposite of the individual, solipsistic identification with the role that is traditionally supposed to be at the heart of the actor's craft. But fundamentally what this process did was it put us in possession of the whole play. It gave us a feel for the whole structure and the challenges that others faced. It gave us an understanding, in great detail, of where we each fitted into the whole story. But the most distinctive difference between this process and others was that the director did not give us her interpretation. She constrained us from doing too much interpretation ourselves and she did not impose her own. Almost every director I had worked with until then had relished the ritual of the first-day speech, when they eloquently (or otherwise) discourse on their view and interpretation of the play and its meaning.

Knowledge is power, they say. Unlike many directors I had worked with up till then, this process properly empowered us. We all knew what we all knew and crucially there was a space where the leader's vision of the project's direction would normally be; the creative possibility was open and there for all of us to explore.

But it was a risk. Whatever happened in the rehearsal room after that, as we got down to the business of rehearsing the interpretation of each scene, the director was working with a cast in possession of the whole piece. The vision felt as if it was up for grabs. What this director did was to assert their authority (their right to "author" our efforts), not by expounding their "vision" of the outcome but by establishing the community that would do the interpreting. She was in a sense the lawmaker. And the community she created was one where there was a clear understanding of each other's role and an equality of status before the task in hand.

The real prize, "What are we to do?" – what would this production be like? – was unknown to us. We thought she might know, but it seemed clear that she was probably in the same place as us and was embarking on this project with a similar lack of clarity about the exact nature of the outcomes. This was tremendously exciting to me as an artist. My remit was expanded beyond trying to please the boss, to trying to work with the boss to find what this huge, problematic play that we were attempting could be.

She may have had very clear ideas about what she wanted various scenes to finally look like. She had already exercised a massive amount of structural control by hiring who she had hired. King Lear was a bristling, pop-eyed 35-year-old, for instance, which was already going to nudge the production in a particular direction, but the strongest factor here was that she was not using the "vision thing" to direct us. The vision was elusive and we all understood that it was yet to be found. Her authority, besides the title and her own quiet strength of personality, lay in the culture she had created, in the rules of the community of which she was the figurehead and lawgiver.

As the rehearsals progressed we had of course to make decisions about what was to be. But again, having established her position as the author of the community, my recollection of the rehearsal process after that is that she spoke very little.

As usual in a rehearsal, the actors would begin a stumbling interpretation of the scene and then grind to a halt. At this point it is usually the case that people sit about trying to discuss what went wrong and plan what they might do next. In this production, and notably in other productions when the outcome was successful, there was very little of this. We would all stop and look to her for some guidance and she would say very little. She might think a bit and then she'd generally just make a suggestion that we try it again in another specific way, or attempt another objective with it.

There was very little interpretation; there was very little discussion of "what went wrong and why"; there was just thought and then moving on. I should say here that of all the directors I have worked with over the years, I think she had the most intense aura of concentration. She sat composed and contained, leaning forward on her chair watching with a breathtaking intensity of concentration. Somehow you knew that she missed nothing: that she had seen all and noted all, good or bad, and if she did not draw it to your attention you need not worry.

This is a very interesting phenomenon. There is something profound about people who pay attention and speak little; it is a phenomenon that is diminishing all around us. There is much talk of listening skills but this goes deeper than that. There was in this director, and in the rules of the community she established, a profound sense that you were being observed and noted in an entirely positive way. It was almost the diametric opposite in feel of the idea of performance monitoring or surveillance that I see in business. Although you knew that what you were doing was being observed and noted, it was not being judged. Or rather it was being judged only in relation to its usefulness in advancing the production.

One felt that she was looking only for originality and insight and that however much of that you could produce she would use. She was not at all bothered or distressed by all the other stuff you did that was not so good. And yet this intuited selectivity somehow set you free. If your crapness was not an issue you could relax; all you needed to focus on was trying to come up with great stuff because then (very rarely) you would get a grin or a compliment. But in my recollection she was never negative in her guidance and direction.

Her process encouraged us to focus on the detail of the next action and to entirely trust the author and the audience to get the big picture and do the work of apprehending the deeper and wider truths of the play. We were put in complete possession of the details of the narrative and the language of the text but one of the constraints she applied when doing this was that interpretation was forbidden. This big work was not ours; it was the audience's.

CHAPTER 5

Hierarchy and Status Games

Visiting India

When I was seventeen I saw a production of *Much Ado About Nothing* by the Royal Shakespeare Company. It was set in the British Raj in India. As I watched the story unfold, I became aware of a sense of heat, of desultory conversations on verandas and a permeating unavoidable feel of India, smells, colors, a subtle ambience, a feeling that I was there, had been transported to another place.

As I watched I became aware that this powerful effect was generated not just by the lighting and the costumes but by the minor characters, the servants, the "spear-carriers" – the actor who came on in a scene almost unnoticed, to plump the cushions and offer a drink when a principal protagonist entered.

This was ensemble playing: a unity of commitment to the spirit of the play that meant that every action of every actor was informed with the same detail, professionalism and passionate commitment to the ideas of the performance. Whether the actor had one line in the whole play or whether they carried the bulk of the narrative, they were as equals in their concentration on the task in hand.

This is the kind of commitment and focus that all organizations crave, but in order to achieve it there needs to be very a specific process in place. In the theater this is loosely termed the ensemble approach: a way of working together that highlights the task, above the status, or roles, of the individuals and springs from an intense and committed level of trust. Getting this trust is the essential first step in the process. Without it nothing can grow.

The key is in understanding the nature of the trust that develops in ensemble work. It is not necessarily the trust of long years; it can be achieved quickly between relative strangers; it does not depend on long experience – but it does require emotional strength, and an experience of humility, even of humiliation. Actors understand what it is to lower their emotional defenses, to allow others space and to experience the simple trust of giving and receiving.

The truth is that for the purposes of working together you do not need to know someone, or even to like them, to trust them profoundly. But you do need to learn and practice some basic emotional disciplines to make it work. This level of unquestioning trust of a relative stranger is usually forged in disaster; floods, wars and accidents bring out this fundamental altruism in us. Catastrophe seems to awake in us an ability to bond with whoever we meet, in a way that is not possible when we feel no immediate threat to the survival of the group.

At its most banal, the discipline of the ensemble is the discipline of good manners; it is rooted in humility, restraint and mutuality. The surprising truth is that if you all agree to surrender control then action emerges, abundantly and creatively. If you all agree to indulge one another then no one is indulgent; all become energized by the task in hand because the space is no longer taken up with the struggle of egos. As a senior manager of a major international financial consultancy said to me, "If we could get rid of egos we'd make millions." The trust required for ensemble working is not the trust of "Would I trust this person with my life, or my wife, or my money?" It is the trust of "Do we both want to see this work well done? "Can I trust them for this moment, in this place, with these thoughts of mine?" It is a limited contract for the workplace only.

That sounds superficial and contingent, but it is not so. It is appropriate and no less profound for that. It helps to maintain your sanity in an ever changing, constantly renewing workplace. But it cannot, paradoxically, be shallow or cynical. The fact that it is limited does not mean it is not true. But it is perhaps real with the paradoxical reality of art. Real in the sense that a novel can stir real tears, that oilpaint on canvas can seem to smile. And of course the best way to learn how to do a thing is to practice it. Practicing trusting in the limited and mechanical way that theater exercises seem at first to encourage teaches the skills that may lead to deep trust emerging as it naturally does over time and with long acquaintance.

The block to trust is relative status. All social animals naturally evolve hierarchies. Knowing where you fit in the hierarchy is essential to survival. Loners die out. When you have found a place, you can relax. But hierarchies are mobile; they are constantly changing and being renegotiated depending on the group's needs, and so there is constant competition and renegotiation of places. This leads to status games. We play them all the time. They take up most of our energy and attention whatever we are doing. We only feel we can relax and trust one another and get on with something when these games are resolved – when we suspend the status games.

Playing status

I am in a room with twenty teachers from the Midlands. They have come to a workshop to learn techniques for the teaching of Shakespeare in schools. The scene we are working on is from The Tempest. *The two characters, Prospero the powerful magician and Ariel his magical servant, are having a row about the chores that Ariel has to complete and Ariel is arguing about his terms and conditions of employment.*

"Let me remember thee what thou hast promised ... "

Prospero is reminding him who is boss:

"What is't thou canst demand? ... "

The teachers read through the scene and begin to act it out in pairs playing the two roles. They all go quickly to the obvious interpretation. There are a lot of grand Prosperos with imaginary cloaks giving orders to cringing servants. It looks like amateur night.

We decide to have a talk and I introduce the idea of status:

"Who's in charge?"

Prospero of course. But does he have the emotional high ground? Doesn't Ariel actually have the magic power? And Prospero made him a promise, didn't he?

OK. He has a case.

Status is not the same as hierarchy. Status, in theater terms, is negotiated moment to moment between the characters in the scenes. It is a flow of the energy between them. It is about who is winning and who is yielding, who is dominant and who is submissive. It is about power.

I suggest that they all try the scene again but this time use a chair:

"Put Prospero up on the chair towering over Ariel and then swap over – try the scene with Ariel up on the chair and Prospero running around beneath him."

They have a go and all the scenes are transformed. The subtlety of the relationship is much clearer. Prospero seems peevish and pedantic when his physical position is lowered.

And the dignity and strength of Ariel's moral position becomes clearer when he is literally higher up than Prospero. The scene begins to yield its secrets.

I came across the idea of status as an acting tool when working with Max Stafford Clark at the Royal Shakespeare Company. His background at the Royal Court Theater connected him with Keith Johnstone and a body of work developed there in the 1970s. Max used status throughout the rehearsal process, urging the actors to look at the dialog in status terms. Lower it, raise it. Compete for lower status. Take your status down a notch; play a ten to his king.

He used playing-cards extensively in a series of exercises that I now use often with businesses. Inviting people to interact and play the status given by the playing-card. Oddly this is not only possible for non-actors to do but any group of people can do it with extraordinary accuracy. In fact is seems it is not just an acting tool. It is the way in to a code of human behavior. I am coming to believe that it might be one of the most fundamental factors in the way people interact.

A group of people are milling about in a room pretending to have a cocktail party. They are chatting to one another and then moving on to introduce themselves to someone else or break into another conversation. It looks a bit forced and some of the conversations are oddly stilted. As you watch, you notice that some of the people look unusually insecure: they don't hold eye contact, they shuffle their feet and look down; others eyeball each other almost aggressively. The exercise ends and they discuss their responses:

- *"I couldn't keep hold of the conversation – I kept losing the thread."*

- *"The non-eye-contact-holders looked shifty."*

- *"I thought they were rude."*

- *"I found the eye contact to eye contact a bit aggressive."*

This is a classic status exercise, similar to ones described in the work of Keith Johnstone. The only instructions to the group were that half the group had to maintain eye contact all the time during their conversations and the other half could only maintain eye contact for a count of two before breaking and looking down. No other instructions were given, apart from the intention to talk to every other person in the group.

The curious thing is that this simple change in body language cascades a whole set of other responses. The eye-contact-avoiders instinctively begin to exhibit other low-status behavior. They cross their arms in front of themselves, they shuffle their feet, they frown and touch their faces when talking. And the eye-contact-holders the same: the men face off to one another, legs planted firmly apart and head slightly back.

The group are struck by two things. First; how for most of them the low-status behavior is difficult and uncomfortable to adopt, but also that there is an emotional context to it. The change in physical behavior brings emotion with it. The non-eye-contact-holders feel shifty and insecure. The high-status people feel that they are indeed shifty or rude, that they may be hiding something. The emotional context of their conversations is changed and rapidly becomes self-reinforcing. The small alteration in physical behavior makes the participants feel differently about each other and about themselves.

And yet these are not actors. No "acting" is required. This is at the root of a profound misunderstanding about the nature of acting and how theater achieves its effects. Acting is not about pretending emotions you don't feel. It is, at its heart, about mimicry. In its oldest and most profound roots it is about dissembling, putting on the mask of another's behavior and style. Putting on the mask invokes feelings in the audience which feed back to the wearer of the mask and so in a self-reinforcing loop can intensify the emotion for both actor and audience. The effect of this is profound. And so also are the implications for how we are.

One of the interesting difficulties with acting has emerged from the relatively recent idea of character, the idea that we are types, that we have immutable humors as the Elizabethans had it, or a knowable and realizable psychology that, if only we could understand it and live it, we would somehow become our true, innate immutable and authentic selves. For an actor it is very disturbing to discover that acting really is possible. You can be "someone else" so completely that to all intents and purposes you *are* them. The experience of acting teaches you the extent to which we are social constructs.

We create status by the way we interact with one another. Status is negotiated between people from moment to moment. Shifts in relative status between us provoke strong emotions. We feel a whole range of different emotions that are engendered by how we feel about our status: anxiety if we are losing status, aggression if our bid for higher status is opposed, shame if we loose it, magnanimity when it is given to us (or at least this is how it feels if you are a man).

These are not necessarily the motivators of our thoughts and actions; they are the unavoidable context of all our face-to-face communications. And a lot of them are triggered by body language alone. This is profoundly odd. It means that we are often responding emotionally to status signals that are mistakes, or caused by other things. We constantly misinterpret these signals because our emotional responses to them are almost completely unconscious. We feel the response and then create a narrative about the other person to explain the feeling that has been provoked. These stories are often quite wrong.

The giant's robe on the dwarfish thief

When I first started working as an assistant director at the Royal Shakespeare Company, I was having the time of my life. I was working on a major new production of *The Winter's Tale* with some wonderful actors. Each day in the rehearsal room was a revelation and my head was full of the responsibilities of my new role and the teeming questions that my first experience of directing raised. After a couple of weeks in my new role I was suddenly summoned to the producer's office for a meeting. I was unsure what to expect, but sensed from her style when she asked me to meet her that all was not well.

I sat down and was at once sure I was in trouble.

"Look," she said, "I don't know what is going on in the rehearsals but you've got to hide your feelings better. You're undermining the cast. They can tell you think the rehearsals are crap and they resent it."

I was dumbfounded.

"It isn't crap," I said, "It's going wonderfully well."

"Well they are convinced you hate it. You come out of rehearsals scowling; you won't look them in the eye. They can tell you loathe it. They need you to look confident even if you think it's rubbish."

The penny dropped.

I was preoccupied. I was nervous about doing my new job well; I had a hundred new and worrying responsibilities and at the end of each rehearsal I had been shooting out of the door with a worried frown on my face. When I am thinking, my face looks as if I am worried. It's just the way my face happens to be. People misinterpret it all the time. The actors, with their natural anxiety about the quality of their early work in shaping the play, were reading this as clear, incontrovertible evidence, that whatever I might say, it was clear from the mask I wore that I thought that they were doing badly and I was worried. I was worried: but not about them. It was my first experience of the power of the mask when attached to the face of someone in an elevated position in a hierarchy.

There are number of things that this story illuminates.

I had failed to appreciate that in becoming an assistant director I had changed my position in the hierarchy and that the status others attributed to me was higher than that of an actor. My inner status, however, the status I felt, and therefore was playing out, had dropped. I was in a new job, unconfident, anxious, green and inexperienced. The previous season with the company I had been an actor with a lifetime's experience (I got my first paid job as an actor at the age of 12), taking leading roles and practicing my craft as I had done for years. In *that* role, I was a confident and experienced professional; my inner status and my position in the extant hierarchy were roughly in accord. In my new job there was a tension between the status I felt and was showing, and my position in the hierarchy.

This tension is one of the most interesting things about status, both as a tool to illuminate the performances of actors and as a source of insight into how we are in the theater of life. There is no simple connection between our position in the social hierarchy, the status we feel, the status we try to project, and the status people attribute to us. It is this disconnection that is at the base of much of what is tragedy and comedy in life and in plays. Shakespeare illustrates this particularly well.

You could say that tragedy and comedy are just two aspects of status play. Tragedies are stories in which the main character loses their high position in the hierarchy and is obliged to play low-status. King Lear is reduced to the-status of a "foolish fond old man." Macbeth, who slaughters his way to the throne, is then reduced to the status of a "dwarfish thief" inside a "giant's robe." And Hamlet is obsessed with his inability to play the status required of his position as Prince of Denmark. The comedies are the obverse of this. They center on stories in which people of low status in the social hierarchy aspire to – or usurp – high status; servants who dress up as their masters. Women (low-status in Shakespeare's day) impersonate men. Foolish servants dream of their mistress being in love with them. A donkey becomes the lover of the Queen of the Fairies.

Hierarchy and clear gradations of status defined Elizabethan society. People were obliged to display status behavior that was in keeping with their rank in the social hierarchy. Life was still highly ritualized. Any public gathering was naturally a ritual of social display. It was immediately obvious from their clothing and gestures who was high and who was low. But Shakespeare was writing in apocalyptic times for the social hierarchy. For the first time since the Norman Conquest of England in the eleventh century, the merchant class was beginning to usurp power, wealth and land from the hereditary aristocracy. The Great Chain of Being, the medieval hierarchy that had dominated people's thinking for centuries, was beginning to fall apart. The line of God's creation that ordered all living things from God, through the archangels, through the different ranks of man, to the higher animals then down to dogs and worms – each in its place, and each a fixed and permanent distance from the divine – all this was being turned upside-down.

Within decades of Shakespeare's death the parliament of England had killed their king and established a commonwealth. There was a terrifying force being unleashed, a final uncoupling of hierarchy from status. The effects of that apocalyptic century are still being felt. We have a culture in the West where the Enlightenment ideas of equality of rights and opportunities are embedded in our social and political structures, but we still play status games and we still need to know where we stand relative to one another. But now we have to find it out by other means. All is negotiable and nothing is clear. Making an organization "flat," or asserting equality of rights and opportunities in law, does not seem to remove this need for us (and particularly for men) to negotiate our relative status with those around us from moment to moment.

I introduced the games of status to some actors from the Piccolo Theater in Milan. They were working on the early scenes of Macbeth. Noble Macbeth and his friend Banquo are returning to court after a great success in battle, to be duly thanked and perhaps rewarded by the wise old King Duncan.

There was small throng of actors in the rehearsal room. The king was doing king acting and the others were doing courtier acting, posing and bowing at the king. We played around a while with different versions of the scene but it was dull. It was a cliché; no one looked like anything but a cartoon version of what a child might think a court was like. Then we did some work on status. The cast ordered themselves into a hierarchy with a king at the top and the different ranks of courtiers in a procession behind him. I encouraged them all to play their rank, to show their position in the hierarchy by the way they behaved – let the status they play be the same as their position in the social hierarchy. It looked like a play.

Then I encouraged them to repeat the scene exactly. Do exactly the same things – help the king to his chair, talk to their fellows just as before – but this time choose a status opposite to their rank. People in the middle stayed much the same but the characters at the extreme ends of the social hierarchy began to play a status opposite to their rank. The servants began to swagger nonchalantly around; the king slumped in a feeble, anxious heap in his chair, barely able to get up without assistance. The high-ranking courtiers looked insecure, paranoid, the middle-ranking courtiers watched with steady confident gaze. At once the scene was rippling with life. There were fascinating cross-currents and tensions. The high-ranking courtiers seemed vulnerable; the low-ranking courtiers might have been waiting for their moment. Suddenly the scene seemed authentic, rich with subtle drama and flows of energy and power.

The tension between our rank and our status fuels our social interactions. We feel obliged very often to play the status that our rank implies. Interestingly, truly powerful and charismatic people seem to be liberated from this game. They can be anything, they are "disarming," they undercut, or won't play, the status game; they are free to exhibit whatever status they like; those that can do this well are often the most charismatic and successful leaders. This uncoupling of rank, or position in the hierarchy, from status as negotiated and signaled moment to moment with others, is at the core of the illusion of leadership.

Hierarchy and status: the tree-house game

A number of managers have been shuffled into groups. There are about seven in each group and they have been playing with the idea of status all morning. I can give any one of them a playing-card and say "Talk to me and play the status on the card," and they can do it. Although they are not actors, they can play and distinguish the difference between someone playing a five and someone playing a seven. They have got pretty good at it.

I fix the pack and then deal out a playing-card to each participant.

"Now you are going to have to do some acting," I say. "I want you to pretend that you are all seven years old." There are some laughs. Some groans.

"I want you to imagine that you are group of seven-year-old children and you are going to build a tree house. You can use the chairs and tables if you like but I want you to improvise that scene and each one of you must play the status on your card relative to the rest of the group and, play it as accurately as you can. Your objective is to play your status throughout the improvisation and to try and work out the status of the other players relative to you."

The groups get to work, gradually relaxing and beginning to enjoy the silliness and the simplicity of the challenge. The people with high-status cards strut around giving orders to their playmates. The very low-status players sit shyly at the side. They look like groups of kids.

But the cards are rigged. Some of the groups are almost entirely composed of high-status players. All the people were given high cards: kings, jacks, queens. Some groups are almost all low-status and a few have a mix, a hierarchy of status from low to high. The improvisations continue, and different stories begin to emerge.

In the high-status groups there is a lot of noise. Three or four of the "children" in the group are shouting at each other. In the low-status group all the "children" are sitting on the ground, muttering shyly to one another. Nothing is getting done. The exercise ends and each group easily identify the relative status of each member of the group.

But the stories are interesting. Of all the groups, only the one with a status hierarchy is standing next to a pile of chairs – the tree-house they were asked to build. In the high-status group, activity was blocked by arguments. In the low-status group no one would begin. Only in the mixed group, where there was a confident, high-status child with support from middle-status children able to coerce or include the low-status children was the task completed. We need hierarchy to get things done.

But the uncoupling of "status" from hierarchy is a complex thing. Talking to a Dutch colleague recently I was struck by a remark of hers.

I mentioned including "support staff" in strategy meetings. "Ah, yes," she said, "English PAs. They are wonderful. You tell them to do something, they do it. In Holland you have to sit down and explain your reasons for ten minutes and then they tell you they have other priorities."

This lifts the lid on a complex area. Not only is the relationship between status and hierarchy different in different cultures; the game is played to different rules. People at the top of Japanese hierarchies are culturally required to exhibit extremely low-status behavior while at the same time being given extremely high status by their subordinates (although this is changing today). To Westerners this can offer a totally confusing set of signals. Obviously in Holland workplace equality is more of a felt reality than in England, and people lower down in the hierarchy will confidently play high-status in conversation with their boss. In America things are on the face of it more straightforward. Bosses swagger and boss but are constantly challenged by people below them. People are better at accepting equal status in the workplace, but a culture of social mobility means that competition for higher-status positions is ferocious, with the result that status behavior is generally very clearly and vigorously displayed. But these crude cultural differences are not the point. Given a few days' training and the right conditions to practice, people can quickly be taught how to exhibit high- or low-status behavior. Anyone can be taught to play anything, and given the right conditions they will get away with it.

Successful leaders and well-functioning teams play status as a game. They are easy about adopting the status behavior required to get the task done. They will happily take on whatever role they are needed for (Whatmore 1999). Hierarchies assemble around the needs of the task in hand, and position in those hierarchies is fluid and changeable. This kind of flexibility often emerges naturally in extreme crisis. People abandon their personal status obsessions for the pressing needs of the group as a whole. What seems to happen in organizations is that issues of status and hierarchy are more important than anything else. People are obsessed by their relative positions in a way that they are not when they are away from work, and much of the reward and punishment put in place by crude management practice reinforces this obsession. Our inability to separate relative status from position in the hierarchy can cripple us. Competitive individualism as a cultural norm reinforces it.

Briefing the general

It is surprisingly rare to meet a person of lofty position in the social hierarchy who does not seem, in the flesh, to be less than we had anticipated. Filmstars and monarchs have a depressing tendency to be smaller, older and uglier than expected. We not only display status signals ourselves; we project them onto others. Paradoxically, people who are high-status and also exhibit high-status behavior are often universally disliked. People feel most comfortable talking to others who are just below them in the status they exhibit. A large gap between the status signals that people exhibit produces powerful emotions in both parties. Yet sometimes we can be disappointed when someone high up in the hierarchy doesn't display the obvious signals we would expect.

Things become even more difficult when groups of about the same position in the hierarchy have to work together in a team. Relative status becomes vital. People (men particularly) constantly need to assert their position in the fear that if they do not they will permanently lose status and drop down the organizational hierarchy. They cannot feel secure until they know where they are in the pecking order. For short periods and in limited areas, people will be happy to lower their relative status to facilitate the group, but they will not drop it for long. They will eventually have to reassert themselves or suffer. This means that progress is constantly thwarted by status games, office politics, rows, grandstanding and so on. In most organizations people are as obsessed with status as the Elizabethans were, and office life can be a daily round of minor farce and minor tragedy.

The increasing amount of assessment and surveillance that people are subject to at work makes people more and more conscious of their every interaction. People are so plagued by the anxiety to "perform" that they feel obliged to show that they are feisty, committed, energetic full of ideas. They are constantly putting on a good show to impress the assessors (who, increasingly, may be anyone and everyone they work with). They can never be offguard and they cannot afford to be the one who only listens for three meetings in a row, even when in order to get things done that may be the most helpful contribution they can make. It could look like low-status behavior. Remember, people read and respond to these signals largely unconsciously; they are not good guides to the reality of a person's inner state.

A person's silence could be interpreted as indifference, disinterest, boredom, sulking or profound thought; it's not easy to know for sure, and so there is an anxiety to clearly exhibit, all the time, the kind of assertive, high-status contribution that people hope is the required target behavior to keep their position. But of course if everyone is playing high-status there can be no play in any true sense and nothing can get done.

In the army, life is very much simpler. The ranks are so clearly defined and displayed that it is much easier to separate the rank on the sleeve from the status negotiation in the conversation. For some of the time in the army people display the status that goes with their rank. The closer in rank, the more vigorous the display. Generals yell at each other (behind closed doors) – private soldiers beat each other up in carparks after a night drinking. But between the ranks there is the possibility for real creative leadership. The hierarchy allows power to flow extremely efficiently when a task needs to be done, but also allows for the game to be suspended when creativity and innovation are required. The British Army has only relatively recently embedded this understanding in its training and increasingly operates this distinction deliberately.

If rank is clear (between men) then suspending it for creative purposes is easy. Here is an email I received from a junior officer in Iraq in 2005:

> I have been getting more involved at higher level planning as well and had to give a briefing to a Major General a couple of days ago which was an experience. He was very relaxed about it and he seemed genuinely interested in my opinions about the future for the operations in our area. He also wanted to meet some of the aircrew but they had all been taken off for an emergency briefing when he turned up so he was stuck talking to me. It also seems that in true army style, everything I thought I was doing over the next six months has totally changed. Firstly I will be back in the UK around the 27th November which is about two weeks earlier than I thought.

It is worth looking closely at what is going on here.

The junior officer is clearly flattered and nervous about the difference in rank but reports (with a degree of relief it seems) that the general "seemed genuinely interested in my opinions." His first impression is that the general "was very relaxed." The general even wanted to meet some of the aircrew (even more junior in rank) and, in conclusion, despite the relaxed exchange that seems to have taken place, the news was that everything has changed, that what is emerging requires that everyone alters what they are doing in response to what is unfolding in the theater of operations and that we are all going to have to adapt.

It is impossible to know what was going on inside the senior officer's head, but either he was genuinely interested and aware that a junior officer in the field will have vital information about things that he may not be able to see, or else he was not really interested at all, but was still able to convey that he was interested with enough conviction to make the junior officer feel proud and valued for his contribution to shaping the "big picture." From the description, it is clear that the senior officer was making efforts to remove the stress from the encounter; he was able to drop the status that goes with his senior rank, and by lowering his own status to raise the junior officer to a place where they were "equal before the task" – the task in this case being to have a creative conversation about strategy in the sector.

But of course most people don't want to be in the army. And we have spent the last two hundred and fifty years trying to break down and liberate ourselves from the bonds of unquestioned rank and hierarchy.

How then do we get around the problems of the status game?

A way of overcoming the potential for deadlock in an "equal" society with a status free-for-all is by ensemble working. One definition of an ensemble could be a group who agree to suspend hierarchy and status games for the purposes of getting things done. Many directors today will not proceed until they have spent a great deal of time creating an ensemble, preparing the team with games and exercises that teach the behaviors that will permit a group to recognize and suspend the behaviors that cascade from the fact of hierarchy and the compulsion to display status.

Sex and status games: invisible women

But in humans (and the other higher apes) there is a difference between the sexes in the way this game is played and experienced. There is very good evidence that men and women respond differently and play the status game differently from the moment they become socialized at the age of three or four. In general men enjoy competing for a place in a hierarchy and are not really comfortable until they have found one. Women, in general, enjoy arranging equal-status groups that others are excluded from or included in. Most male–male conversations contain elements of status competition and most female–female conversations contain elements of status amelioration. This fundamental difference in status play has profound consequences for mixed-gender groups and there is much interesting research around this issue. (I would particularly recommend Deborah Tannen's work in this area; see Tannen 1991 and other books by her.)

I saw this difference illustrated with extraordinary force when I was invited to do some work on communication for a major bank. I was encouraged to work with female-only groups as part of drive to support diversity in the organization. We played the status game described above where the group are given playing-cards and invited to organize themselves into a hierarchy, illustrating the exact differences between the ranks by body language alone.

When I am running this exercise normally, as facilitator I can usually tell by watching the ensemble when they have begun to group themselves with people of the same rank. I can also usually tell at a glance who in the group are holding the very high cards and who are holding the very low ones (the middle ranks are always more difficult to discern). But this time, as I watched the group of twenty or so women in the room playing the game with exactly the same degree of commitment and enjoyment as any other group I have worked with, I realized I could not see who was high-ranking and who low. I could not tell when to intervene and encourage them on to the next part of the exercise. As a man observing a group of women, I could not see them playing the game. I ran the exercise to its completion as usual, and the group lined themselves up as in any group I have played the game with, and they were able to work out their relative status with exactly the same degree of accuracy as any group I have worked with in the past, but I had not been able to see them do it.

When an all-male group, or a mixed group, are invited to play around with status games they exhibit a more extreme range of behaviors than an all-female group. To my male eyes, sensitive to and looking for hierarchy signals, the female group looked as if no one was displaying behavior much higher than a nine or much lower than a five. Men process status signals in the context of position in a hierarchy. I was not just looking to see what status they happened to be showing, to asses their mood and how I could interact with them; I was using their body language signals subliminally to rank them relative to me, as all men do with other men. Could some of the difficulty women experience progressing successfully to the higher levels in some organizations be no more than the fact that they do not naturally display high-status body language signals to the group? At some crude and unconscious level, men simply do not see the signals that women give out and respond instead to whoever is giving out the highest-status signals.

The problem is compounded of course by the fact that women notice and respond (often negatively) to the kind of very high-status body language men are comfortable with (such as swaggering and shouting). The net result must be that even in a mixed group everyone will notice and respond to those who give out the high-status signals, and they are less likely to be the women. These (high-status) individuals may not necessarily advance further or faster through an organization, but they will take up more time and attention than the others, which will have a net effect on relative progress.

I am talking here about the physical signals only, quite divorced from the power, experience or content of what people may say. We do not need to understand motives or connect with the content of what people say to make a strong response to the status signals they display. Men are at an advantage if they are tall, still, deep-voiced and un-talkative, for example. Whatever kind of ability they may have, they will be attended to more than people with other attributes. They will be given the illusion of leadership.

Is dissembling a sin?

The thorny question then is what to do about this. I have been confronted in no uncertain terms by the inappropriateness of "training women to act like men" – although this is a strategy that many women have used to advance in organizations – Margaret Thatcher being a noted example. Watching her behavior at the beginning and at the end of her twelve years in power is an object lesson in displaying high-status body language. Obviously the better path is to out this behavior and show it for what it is – a highly evolved and subtle language that we are largely unconscious of and can all benefit from understanding both how to read and how to deliver appropriately.

There is already much work out there in this area from neurolinguistic programming through high-pressure selling to negotiation and presentation skills training. All use elements of this craft to develop people's range of displayed behaviors. And it is all fraught with difficulty in a moral sense. If we change the signals we display consciously, are we being false, artificial and manipulative? This is the deep fear of dissembling, so acute in Renaissance times that actors were considered to be mortal sinners and could not be buried on consecrated ground.

But what of the therapist who presents the perfect listening pose and carefully and artificially tempers their tone, body language and eye contact in order to help a patient to express some painful or liberating truth that they have never been able to share before? What of the teacher, whose stern and forbidding mask is loved and feared in equal measure by pupils that are liberated into a state of disciplined yet eager concentration in a lesson by a gifted mentor? Police officers conducting interrogations are masters of body language, allowing them to extract information from suspects without recourse to unacceptable threats or behavior. These are dissemblers too, but to great ends. As a parent, the greatest gift my training as an actor gave me was the skill to use a voice and intonation that would get my young children quickly off to bed with energy and certainty that they must do it, but without fear or guilt and the ensuing tears.

People, and other animals that live in groups, cannot function unless they know their place. It doesn't even seem to matter much what that place is for people to be content. Most of the communication that passes between people is signaling this. The often unspoken, almost unconscious context of everything we say and do is mediated by this need to find out where we stand relative to one another. The extreme and obvious hierarchies have been undermined by centuries of politics and social reform predicated on the profound assertions of the Enlightenment, namely that all men are created equal, that human rights are universal, that we are all more alike than we are different and that we should aspire to a condition of absolute equality of status.

But this aspiration seems to have increased "status anxiety." Equality of opportunity has not made our obsession with relative position in a hierarchy go away; we have just reasserted it in more subtle forms. We no longer have sumptuary laws that dictate what clothes each rank of society is allowed to wear, as they did in medieval times, but go into any office and people know who is higher up than whom; who is in, who is out, who is more powerful than they seem. It is those of us in a mêlée of alleged equals where hierarchy is discouraged or denied that find ourselves obliged constantly to test the water to find out where we are.

And of course hierarchy is essential for getting things done.

CHAPTER 6

Masks and the Sense of Self

The immutable self

There is an idea about that we are types, that we have immutable humors, or a knowable and realizable psychology and that, if only we could understand it and live it, we would somehow become our true, innate immutable and authentic selves: the "real me" behind the mask of parent, lover, maverick. For an actor it is very disturbing, and in some cases it drives people literally mad to discover that acting really is possible. You can be "someone else" – so completely, that to all intents and purposes you are them. Working with masks allows one to see that at the heart of this dilemma is play, we are playing at these things and that there is no harm in that, because truthful acting, great playing, can only come from a place of deep humility. Great acting is not about ego, it is about humility; it is about the absence of ego and that is a morally sound place. There is no danger to the soul in being a consummate performer. The danger lies in believing you are the mask.

The American "Method", devised by Lee Strasberg in the 1930s and used to train actors ever since, is particularly interesting in this context. The Method comes from a different place than the rigorous "outside – in" approach of the older European mask tradition. It is strongly rooted in the work of the Russian actor and director Stanislavski, who developed it in a response to the movement in writing for the theater at the turn of the century when the idea of realism and naturalism were being explored by great masters such as Chekhov and Ibsen.

They were seeking a new theater that was true to life, that broke away from the mannered accretions of the theater of the nineteenth century, where melodrama and spectacle had sucked the humanity and power from much theatrical production (much as the Hollywood blockbuster of the 1980s and 1990s weakened, in the end, the dramatic powers of cinema.) And they were also writing at the same time as Freud and Jung and the other founders of modern psychiatry were developing their ideas. The meeting of these ideas in America in the 1930s, after a visit by the Moscow Arts Theater to New York in 1923, set off an explosion of creativity in the American theater that yielded some of the most influential ideas about acting in recent times. The Method school produced legends such as Brando whose power and charisma transformed American cinema. (The irony is that Strasberg rather despised the cinema and was hoping to transform the theater, but his Method proved rather more use for cinema than for the stage.)

In "method acting" there is an attempt to encourage the actor to transform not just the mask of the self but the very "psychology of the self"; to produce not just the effects in the audience that the performance requires but to truly inhabit an alternative psychology. This deeper sense of playing a role is quite harrowing to experience and has yielded a theater that is close to the experience of psychotherapy and not unconnected to it. Actors who attempt this degree of deep transformation do seem to become famously neurotic and strange (including Brando in his later years) and admit that the attempt (as one might expect) may jeopardize their sanity.

We wear masks all the time. When I am at home with my children in scruffy clothes reading to them, putting them to bed, my body language is different from when I am in the coffee break with work colleagues or sitting in a client meeting. All these styles are uniquely mine but they are different and produce different effects. None of this is "me" and yet I have no other existence except the present one. This is the "me" that manifests in the world and for the purposes of the employment contract that is all that matters.

The idea of a deep, fixed, authentic self that is somehow buried in us, of which we are largely unconscious and yet represents "the real me," is a recent construct. In Elizabethan plays the characters say what they are and what they feel, from moment to moment. The audience is not required to infer their inner state from their surface appearance. People in the plays are expected to declare what they feel and who they are, and if they do not they are a dissembler, with a "false face".

Public displays of grief and affection were much more widespread in European society, even until quite recently. It was quite common for members of parliament up to the end of the nineteenth century to weep openly in debates at the news of an English defeat or victory.

Freud and also Jung's idea that we had a deeper, truer, self inside us that we were often blind to (as Oedipus was blind to his own actions) is also a relatively new idea. The migration of this idea into most people's thinking, via popular psychology books and a widespread interest in psychotherapy and psycho-analysis, has led to a generally held belief that we have an authentic self that we have an absolute duty to find, reveal, strengthen and express. That we must be "true to ourselves" and that true self must be expressed freely and openly. This quest has had some unexpected consequences.

It encourages us to examine ourselves constantly for what that true thing might be and therefore to doubt many of our casual, instinctive responses. We no longer heartily trust our own impulses. It has also been interpreted as a license to express openly whatever we find in there, from profound selfishness to pedophilia. "It's in my nature – I can't help myself."

On a more superficial level, but perhaps just as damaging to society as a whole, it has created a culture where the wearing of any social mask, the performance of any social ritual, can be decried as superficial or inauthentic. There is a copy of an old British war-time propaganda poster on the wall of a friend's office. It was posted up in the air-raid shelters during the London Blitz. It reads: "Keep Calm – Carry On." It is an exhortation to perform: to mask your fear and panic and continue with the actions of normality in spite of your inner state, and, in that performance of courage, to find courage and to display it, for the encouragement of others.

If you follow contemporary thinking to its logical end and attempt to strip away all "the masks" to reveal the naked beating self, you have a bit of a problem. Psychoanalysis, which at least to some extent purports to do this, is famously unending. We are onion-layered, or, more accurately perhaps, we are infinitely complex and under each layer there is always another just as complex as the one stripped away. The therapeutic process is about stripping away the layers that don't serve you well, and as far as that is possible it is a help. But if we insist on authenticity in the abstract where are we?

The desire to strip away the masks our parents or grandparents wore to get them through the depression of the 1930s and the Second World War (an enterprise in which I was actively engaged in my youth), plus the attack in the 1960s on hypocrisy within and deference towards the "ruling classe," has left us with a suspicion of masks in general and has been compounded, fatally, by a belief in a paradigm imported from the history of science. Namely that, if you go deep enough, you get to the core, the atoms, the "truth." You reveal the fundamental laws that govern everything.

This is most clearly seen in all the nonsense pedaled about memes and such statements as, "We are 'really' only gene-replicating machines." These ideas about "real motives" have metamorphosed into a conventional wisdom that eschews everything that could be called a mask and a general suspicion that what people "really" mean, think or feel is hidden, repressed, or deliberately concealed, and we are only being "real" when we are yelling at each other or weeping (expressing our "real" pain and grief) or ruthlessly pursuing our own self-interest (self-interest being the only fuel that gene-machines can run on) (see Midgely 1985).

All the complex play of appearances in the world is suspect. The result is that the constraints on our behavior that are implied by such phrases in

English as "putting on a brave face," "keeping your chin up" or "showing respect" are regarded as laughable, antique and totally inauthentic behaviors; behaviors that are not merely old-fashioned and reactionary, but false, fake, morally wrong – "not being true to yourself." It is as if circumspection or emotional restraint were some kind of abuse of power.

George Bush famously appealed to this tendency by wearing a mask of simple, folksy openness and simplicity. Tony Blair wore one of deep feeling and stuttering sincerity. What relationship these masks had to their "real selves" I have no idea, but their attempt at "emotional openness" was no less a mask than that of any other leader performing on the public stage. Increasingly, the masks seen in public, in the West at least, are ones of our more raw, undifferentiated and extreme feelings. This may be very honest. We do all really have these feelings, but unfortunately, in every sense, it is uncivilized to display them all the time. Civilization depends on our ability to reign in and *not* display our cruder impulses.

We are all required to perform many different roles in life. These performances are for the benefit of others as well as us. And they are co-created with our fellow actors and with the audience that we seek to entertain, delight, torture or impress. Whatever method we employ, the craft of acting shows that we are all capable of becoming different people; it is only a matter of technique. We can play any role we want. Given the right conditions and training, anyone can become a priest, a torturer or a leader. Whether we do this on stage, or in life, is only a matter of our choices and our circumstances.

Whether we can do it well, or whether our performances are sustainable, is another matter. What we display matters crucially to the effects we have in the world and the response we can expect from others. We need to reflect very deeply on what is "the right" mask for the moment. Great acting teaches us that the right mask is our simple self, responding to the infinitely complex moment with effortless presence.

Clowns and ringmasters: training the masked actor

The training of masked actors is fascinating: and for me, yielded the deepest insight into what acting actually is and raised some profound questions about the authentic self and how we operate in the world. My first contact came with a workshop on clowning.

In the European tradition the clown is a curious figure, probably descended from the masked clowns of the Italian Commedia dell'Arte companies that were around in Shakespeare's time and may even come from an older tradition that goes back directly to the early mummer plays, where religious or traditional stories were acted out at festivals by local people. Some of these clowns or fools may have truly ancient roots that could take us right back to the masked hunter of the cave paintings.

The court fool, the licensed jester of the medieval European court, is a strange idea to us. Their "jokes" as much as we can understand them in Shakespeare and other playwrights of the time, are dreadful or incomprehensible. They are supposed to be wise but come across as arch or incomprehensible. The actors in Shakespeare's company that played these characters are described as clowns rather than fools in his early plays and they seem, in contemporary descriptions, to have used a lot of clowning techniques, among them improvisation, slapstick and pathos, to achieve their effects. As Shakespeare's writing matured and fashions in entertainment changed, he got rid of his clown and started to write roles for wise fools played by actors – a different thing altogether. Today the clown is a well-established character of the circus and the children's party. The accepted masters of this relatively modern tradition of circus clowning are the Russians and the Italians, and the trademark of all clowns is that reduced and minimalist mask the red nose. You can buy one in any joke shop and hold in your hand a very powerful and peculiar device.

My first experience of this power was at a clown workshop hosted by a mask theater company who were looking for new recruits. It was an open audition process that consisted of a week of workshops on clown and mask skills, after which the company were to select two people to join them. I was not among them. The exercise that set me thinking, and has stayed with me ever since, was one of the simplest and most basic in the training of clowns or masked actors.

In essence, the actor puts on their red nose and disappears behind a screen. The audience of fellow students sit on the floor in front of it enclosing a small arena, and the actor emerges from behind the screen to entertain them. But in this traditional form of training, there is an antagonist as well as a protagonist, in the form of the ringmaster. The ringmaster is the interlocutor, the interrogator of the mask and, potentially, the nemesis of the clown. In the exercise, the ringmaster is also the coach, the director, and the teacher of the clown.

The exercise consists of the clown emerging from behind the screen to entertain the audience and the ringmaster directing and teaching the performer by asking the clown questions, by interrogating the mask. The actor responds to the ringmaster's instructions and questions and, in responding, learns, from the audience's reaction, what works and what does not. There are two simple character notes that all clowns have, things about their nature that makes them clowns. One is that they are desperate to please the ringmaster and the other is that they don't want to part from the audience. What else, is for the performer to discover in themselves.

I encountered this exercise after about two days of workshops with the group. We had explored body movement; had tried extremes of movement, looking at the tension states, as they are known; from movement of total relaxation to movement of extreme tension, from walking like a drunk to walking like a paranoid. We had made and explored masks of different types; we had looked at characteristics of movement, leading with different parts of the body, perfecting waddles, struts, skips and shuffles. We were then left some time to develop some minimal style for our own clown. Was he or she sad, bumptious, a showoff?

When we were ready, we all sat cross-legged on the floor in a semi-circle in front of the screen. The ringmaster sat on a chair among us in the audience. And then one by one we donned our red noses and disappeared behind the screen to face our interrogations.

Although I was already not sure if this work was for me, I was keen to please, I wanted to do well, and when it was my turn I stood up and went behind the screen with ideas and ambitions about my performance:

I popped my head round the screen and grinned at the audience.

Silence.

This was a bit of blow. Someone before me in the group had done this and everyone had roared with laughter. I ducked back behind the screen and had a think.

"Are you coming out to say hello?" said the ringmaster.

I didn't know what to do. I waited. I heard the audience laugh. Encouraged, I stuck my head out from behind the screen, grinning madly to get them to laugh again.

Silence.

I stepped out into the space and walked around, doing my clown walk.

Silence.

"What are you doing?" said the ringmaster.

"I'm going for a walk," I said, in my best clown voice.

Silence.

"No you're not. Stand still," said the ringmaster.

I stopped, crestfallen. They laughed.

"Are you going to do something for us?" said the ringmaster.

I was at a loss: I shook my head. They laughed.

"Go on," he said.

I shook my head again and folded my arms to show that "This little clown is not going to obey!"

Silence.

I started walking about, doing "I will not co-operate" acting. The silence deepened into disaster, the audience began shifting with embarrassment. I was dying.

"Stand still!" said the ringmaster, quite firmly.

I stood still. I was beginning to give up. I couldn't get the hang of this. I just felt like a fool. The silence lengthened. I stared at the floor.

"You're not very good at this are you?" said the ringmaster.

This sounded to me like a personal comment, no longer a game. I was shattered. No clown. No acting. I'd been found out. I felt utterly, totally, humiliated, I was never going to get the hang of this, I wanted to leave. The audition was over: I sighed deeply.

"No," I said, "I suppose I'm not."

The audience erupted in howls of laughter. I looked around, utterly bewildered. They laughed again, some helpless now. I was filled with triumph.

They stopped.

The ringmaster's law is iron. The clown must obey, but the profound revelation of this exercise was the experience of standing in front of an audience and not acting – of not trying: of feeling, at full force, the fear that keeps practically everyone off the stage. The fear of standing in front of your peers without any sense of power, or control, or even dignity, and feeling utterly humiliated, utterly humble, and the revelation that, if you are wearing a mask, that is the moment when the mask will work and transform you in the eyes of the audience.

It is when you can really feel like a fool, when you can be completely vulnerable before them, when you can be your naked self, that the audience will trust you. But it is more complex than that. And I did not learn the other side of this strange equation until much later in my career, when, after further training, I had the temerity to try this exercise in the role of the ringmaster. Then you begin to understand how the mask works.

On the face of it, literally, the mask is fixed. It is not a living, mobile, ever-changing face; that "book wherein we read strange matters," the living eyes, the windows of the soul are dead in a mask. The voice may be absent or distorted and the fixed expression forever frowns or scowls or leers. But when you work with a full mask in the exercise above, not just a red nose, it is possible to induce the most astonishing transformations and it becomes clear that the mask and the impact of the performer are created by the context.

The next time I encountered this exercise it was being led by a member of the distinguished British mask troupe, Trestle Theater. An actor was wearing a full mask, covering the whole face, known as naïve mask – a simple, plastic mask, with only two small eye-holes, and an angry scowl painted on it. He was stomping round the arena looking angry.

"You look very cross," said the ringmaster.

(In these masks it is not possible for the actor to speak.) ,

The actor nodded his head vigorously.

"There's no need to be cross ..."

He nodded again, trying to insist.

"Do you know why?" The actor, I could sense, was nonplussed, did not know how to show what he wanted. The masked looked up.

"Someone in this audience is in love with you."

The angry mask began to melt.

"Shall I tell you who it is?"

The angry mask gave a little, tentative, nod and for a second, a look of desperate sweetness was there.

"No, not today" said the ringmaster.

And the angry mask was furious again.

It is hard to convey the delightful shock of this. The plain, fixed, angry face changed and another expression was written there. Of course what is happening here, and in the clown example, is that the audience are creating the life of the mask as much as the actor is. The ringmaster – the interlocutor – the actor and the audience together are co-creating what is to be made of the mask.

When you work with full masks, not just red noses, it is possible to completely change the mask by asking it the right questions. Under the right circumstances the fixed and angry mask suddenly seems to smile, the happy smiling mask looks, for a moment, lost and forlorn. The power of this, what is known as the "counter-mask," in the conditions of the bare, stripped-down performance of the exercise, is truly astonishing.

As I went on in my acting career I began to be convinced that every part of our repertoire of communication operates in this way. Our language operates like a mask; our body language, our position in the social hierarchy, the status we play in different contexts, the words we use, the clothes we wear, all operate like masks. We and our intentions are only a third of what is understood by us. Our audiences and our interlocutors compose the rest of us. We are only a third of what we think we are. The big question for the actor and for anyone performing on the social stage is usually regarded as: "What lies behind the mask?" I am more interested in: "How is this mask working?"

Being Badger

But my own view of "good acting," in the sense of high craft, is slightly different. It is not just about putting on a mask but "becoming" the mask.

This is regarded by people in normal life as spooky or impossible or, most interestingly, as morally wrong. Putting on a "brave face" implies that behind the mask I am still my cowardly, frightened, hopeless, self – that is, the "real" and by implication, the immutable, "me." And so (nowadays) putting on a mask, even if it is a "brave face," is regarded with suspicion; it is inauthentic, fake – like "correct" manners. In method acting, there is an attempt to recall and reenact "real," recovered, memories and feelings of your own that are authentically similar to those required by the role. If you are playing a homicidal maniac, this can be rather disturbing.

Great acting for the stage, where you are working in real time, with a live audience, points you in another direction. It requires you, for a moment (and just for a moment), to forget your past and your "self" and actually, during the time it takes to say those words, to actually "be" Dr Lvov cross, or Hamlet confused. This is what in the jargon they call "being in the moment." It requires you to have a much looser hold on what you "are" and undermines the idea that you have an immutable self. It also requires you not to "act", in the sense of pretending something you have made up. Paradoxically, great actors who can do this trick have a powerful sense of authenticity. What marks them out is that when they are doing this "being" thing they seem most simply, nakedly, themselves.

Sir Michael Bryant – one of the greatest and least well-known of the recent masters – was always utterly scathing about this kind of "inside-out" construction process and there is a story about him that beautifully illustrates this difference of approach. He was in a production of *The Wind in The Willows* at the Royal National Theater in London, in which all the cast were playing different animals. Michael Bryant was playing the Badger. The director had sent everyone out to "research their animal." They had to go to the zoo and look at film and learn the characteristics of the creature they were to perform, so they could construct their "character." They all came back to the rehearsal and each one reported what they had found out. Finally, reluctantly, the director asked Sir Michael to tell the company what he had found out about his animal. "I have discovered," he said, "that all badgers are exactly like Michael Bryant."

This is the secret of great acting.

I believe that the only stance from which to operate truthfully in this theater of life is from that extraordinary place of humility that I visited briefly in the clown exercise. A place where I had surrendered all attempts to force things to go my way but was nevertheless aware, responsive, and still present. I had not left the stage or gone away to hide. I was still out there in front of the audience and responding with honesty to the questions – but it was only in the moment of unmediated and bare-assed truth – when I let go of all my vanity and will, my desire to control and make things happen as I imagined they should – that I achieved the full expression of the role I was playing, of, in that case, the clown, whose job it is to provoke laughter.

What I found later in my acting career was that this holds true of any role you play. This same state of humble surrender – to the play of forces that exist between you, the mask you have chosen, your interlocutor and whatever witnesses may be present – is at the heart of what we call truth in acting, of authenticity, of honesty. It is an egoless place. It is about existing only and completely in the moment, being wholly present with the people in the room. The secret of good acting is not to act at all.

But this discipline does not just apply to performers on the stage. I discovered, when I began leading workshops myself, that this same inner state applies to the ringmaster too. When you are sitting in the director's chair, arms folded, watching the student creep out from behind the screen, you too are bound by this insight. Although you may wear the stern voice and high status of the coach, you too must be operating from that surrendered, unknowing, intensely vulnerable place, to find the right question and deliver it at a time and in a way that will drive the student to that place where they too, can surrender themselves to the situation and succeed.

But this surrender to the moment and to the mask is not to surrender choice. It is the opposite: it allows you all choices. If you understand and accept that the mask you are given as leader is exactly that – a mask – you are free to express your true, momentary, self through it; accepting that what you do, will be interpreted and fed back in ways you cannot control or predict. Some will loathe it, some will laugh and you can be simply present and observe what is unfolding and act accordingly.

Your actions can then be informed more coolly by what is right, what is good, what is useful. People become crippled by the idea that they are, or must become, the mask. "I am a doctor, so I must always be right, I must find out how to behave in a properly 'doctorish' way," rather than: "I am wearing a doctor mask so I must listen and see what is unfolding." This is a more easeful and better place to be.

"I am a teacher so I must always be the one who knows" is not as good as: "I wear the mask of teacher here, so let me listen and see what unfolds." To act well is to be present; to listen and to see and respond to what unfolds. Your audience, by their responses, will show you how the mask is working and guide you in what to do.

I once worked with a group of senior managers in Canada; among them was a man in his late fifties who was the fire chief of a neighboring city. Always very popular with "the boys," he never played that rank stuff with them. They always called him Jim and he was clearly held in great respect and affection by the firefighting teams. But he found himself in a nasty political fight with a bunch of City politicians who did not respect him. For the purposes of City Hall politics this "Call me Jim" performance meant that they disregarded him, thought he was a soft oldtimer who was missing the point. Not hearing his subtle views on the issue in question (which was around the extremely delicate and complex matter of women in the frontline of firefighting services), they saw him as ineffectual, a yesterday's man.

While we were doing work on status games and practicing the different ways relative status could be communicated he had a revelation. He realized that when he was with the City Hall politicians he continued to play the status game in the same way as he did with "his boys." He remained his "authentic self:" he was relaxed and easy and tried to achieve his ends by low-status play. He realized that in the City Hall play he needed to deliver a different performance as fire chief. He needed to keep his cap on, polish his medals and bang his fist on the table – play high-status until the (male-dominated) council listened and were able to hear his views. He was very excited by the work we were doing and during after the lunchbreak he told me that he had tried it out on another group. He told me that he had gone over to another group of delegates attending some totally different event who were having lunch. He had swaggered over and introduced himself, consciously employing all the high-status body language that we had been working on that morning, and told them that he had been watching them and thought they looked like a fine bunch of guys and wanted to know what business they were in. Within minutes he had been invited to join them, the CEO had given him his business card and was sharing his goals and objectives for the company. Jim came back delighted and triumphant. "They didn't even ask me who I was!" he said.

This is not about lack of authenticity but about being aware of the many roles required of us and delivering effective performances, ones that are true to the context. We can change our performance and still be ourselves. An actor is not a different person in different roles. If you watch the same actor in different plays it is always unequivocally them. But the very best ones somehow manage to subsume themselves in the story so that the play or the film's total impact lands on you with full emotional power. It is not about them but them in the context of the unfolding narrative. This is just as true of life as it is of the theater.

The choices you make in playing out your role the objectives you pursue and the tactics you employ from moment to moment are of course a matter of ethics and taste. This view of leadership is focused on the effects you have on others; on the effects of your actions on the audience, or in the world. Actors are trained and practice playing; they are comfortable with all the ranges of behavior that different roles imply. Playing a role does not necessarily require that you think something different; it requires that you wear different habits, adopt different posture, intonation, eye contact and body shape, and that will have various effects. First it will affect how you feel. Second, it will also give out signals that others will read in various ways, signals that may repel or disgust others, or put them at ease. Third, it allows you to influence the status of others.

By adopting low status with people you will automatically raise theirs by contrast. If you play low status but are forthright you will achieve a different effect in the world than if you play low status and are shy. The effect of your actions, your desires, your attempts to affect the world, will yield different results if you operate a low-status mask. And the converse will occur when you pursue the same objectives by the same means, but do it using high-status behaviors. Understanding and being able to play status can radically change how you operate in the real world, just as it illuminates and changes the effect of a scene in a play.

To play around with your status in the real world, rather than in the safety of a rehearsal room, requires confidence and a very strong sense of your aims. And it can be dangerous if you do it badly or for the wrong ends. People will notice and you will be found out. Most politicians employ quite specific acting techniques to achieve their effects on others. High-pressure selling, NLP and many "communication techniques" use these approaches. And the whole idea of acting in this way has a worrying moral implication. It seems to be about deceiving, pretending to be what you are not, to achieve your goals. It is the Elizabethan sin of dissembling, the management of appearances. The illusion of power.

CHAPTER 7

Creativity in Groups

Weird produces wonderful: casting for creativity

In order to tell a good story, to get a rich and creative interpretation of the ideas laid down for you to explore, you need to have variety in the room. When you sit down with a cast of actors at the start of rehearsals you can get a feel for whether it's going to be a good and productive rehearsal just from looking round the room. For example:

It is the first day of rehearsals. Sunlight streams in through the window of a scruffy church-hall.

Here they are:

- *An old woman with a round, smiling face.*

- *A very tall, middle-aged man with long hair in a pony-tail.*

- *A very young-looking girl with a serious frown.*

- *A beaten-looking middle-aged man with a large belly and a fleshy face.*

- *Two young men with baseball caps and strong northern accents.*

- *A thin, pinched, elderly woman with some knitting sticking out of her bag and scarlet-lipstick.*

- *A troubled-looking, dark-haired man, in a leather jacket.*

With a cast like this you know you can tell an interesting story. Theater celebrates the strangeness and the variety of human life, and bringing together a cast of actors as rich and varied as possible will almost always yield a rich result. But actors also bring with them questions of status and of hierarchy. They are the same as everyone else and a theater company is an organization like any other. The people I have described above will bring to the room a variety of experience and different levels of confidence. And these variations will cause dynamics within the group that must be dealt with before creative work can begin.

One of the young actors is fresh from drama school, nervous about their first professional job.

Another of the young actors has been working professionally since they were a child. One of the older actors is a television star who has very little stage experience. Another is a teacher of acting, as well as a performer.

One has a background in dance.

One has a drug problem.

All this variety of life and experience is a resource. But of course, like any group, they will be concerned about their relative status. They will be unconsciously playing all the usual human games to establish a place where they will fit, relative to one another. For the rehearsal, however, you need to be able to access all this variety, all this difference of perspective and perception. If any one of the cast becomes blocked, belittled, inhibited, afraid of how the others will receive their contribution, you will loose the possibility of finding a form for the performance which is passionately shared by all.

So the first thing that must be done, before work begins, is to get rid of these anxieties: to build trust within the group, create an ensemble, where status games are suspended and all the people in the room are engaged with same energy, the same commitment and the same degree of relaxed playfulness. Ensemble games and exercises not only provide actors with an invaluable set of tools for unlocking the complex flows of power that any play is about: they also illuminate the games they play with each other, that may block the rehearsal process itself.

Hair-washing and the puppy game

My wife washes her hair in the morning – for all sorts of good reasons. I can't understand why she doesn't do it in the evenings and give me a break from doing all the stuff with the kids and making the breakfast on hair-washing days. It seems clear to me that it would be sensible to wash it in the evening, when the kids are in bed, leaving the mornings clear. This vision of a better way of doing things bothers me. I can work out that it should be possible but I know I have only part of the picture (I am a bit vague about the sleeping-on-wet-hair problem for example), though I am sure it could be fixed.

As I begin to ponder the problem I am beginning to enter the same creative territory that precedes all innovation. I enter a complex boundary zone where I have the problem and only a visionary fragment of a solution. I could regard this creative problem as my own and take it off to my studio or laboratory and work away at it, trying different ideas, wrestling with the problem until I emerged with a solution to the whole thing and then instruct my wife in how to do it. This might not be a successful approach.

Immediately others are involved we move to another type of creative process. We are no longer in the deep cave of our own imagination. In any group situation, manifesting my vision is not up to me. It's up to my relationships with others; and that is the territory we are mostly in, who have normal lives and are not artists or scientists. How do we work creatively and innovatively when we are working in a team, within a relationship, or within a community of others?

At the heart of the creative process in theater is improvisation. In order to be able to improvise, actors need to be free in the right context. The creative spark that is at the root of improvisation requires that the actor and all those working with the actor be trained to accept and explore their first thoughts. People are wary generally about the idea of "being creative:" they feel it necessitates being original, they think it is to do with cleverness. But creativity, in this context, is just a general term for making things. I say a few words, and someone accepts it. As soon as the gesture is accepted I am free, I have made a start and can begin to play and invent.

If you listen to children playing imaginary games they spend a long time in preparation before they enter the invented space. They always begin from where they are and travel in small steps. Here is a snatch of conversation I noted down from my daughters when they were aged three and six:

"Let's play the puppy game."

"OK."

"I'll be the princess."

"OK."

"I'll be the puppy."

"No, I'll be the puppy."

"Let's be puppies."

"OK."

"OK, let's pretend I'm a puppy and I'm going down stairs." (Going down stairs on all fours.)

"And I'm at the top of the stairs and pretend you go down."

"Yes, and then I get lost."

"Yeah, and I can't find you."

"Yeah, I'll have to be lost."

"Yeah. Let's be lost in the sitting room."

"And I'll be the princess and come and find you."

They are negotiating roles, and even though this is a familiar game they are easing themselves into it. They are grounded in the normal, yet are moving into being able to reframe that normality in a way that will gradually lead them into a creative space. The invention comes later. They almost always, in the early stages, have a time when they are saying the equivalent of: "OK, let's pretend I am standing here and you are standing there." They decide to pretend before they start to invent. They deem their present reality an imaginary one, one that can be transformed any way they like. Then they begin to make inventive offers that are first accepted and then modified.

We are deeply uneasy with this as adults. Schooling and experience make us afraid of creativity. We are taught that it is the stuff of genius and artists, and comes from inspiration and other such nonsense. Children know better. It is a simple and quite banal journey in the mind from where you are now. The thing that makes it possible for my daughters to go together to a different imaginative space is that they say yes to each other. They sometimes need to negotiate the starting premise but they know instinctively that they need to say yes to some early propositions or the game will not unfold. This is the core skill of improvisation, but it requires humility. It depends on the people involved accepting one another's first thoughts.

In the competitive and individualistic world of work, it is very difficult to find a space where some tentative first step will be greeted with an encouraging "yes." Status games, particularly those that involve competing for high status in a group, make this receptivity nearly impossible. It is a very low-status maneuver to go along with the first thing anyone says. But that is what is required if you are to invent together.

It is all much easier if you are alone. If you want to imagine in your head, then this process need not happen. You can daydream away quite happily. The minute you try to make those dreams concrete, however, the problems begin. If you are an artist working alone and you bring your creation to the world, if it is rubbish, it doesn't matter; people won't buy it, or read it and no one is hurt but the artist. But if it is a public policy, or a business strategy, or a plan that involves your partner, it matters a lot. Ensemble co-creation is more than just an effective process, it also a moral and political process. It avoids the onanistic tyranny of the single dream.

There are plenty of directors who get their shows on regardless of the actors. In my experience their work is sometimes so idiosyncratic that the audience's engagement, which is at the heart of good theater, is difficult to achieve. It is less likely to be universal in its appeal. But even when it is great and admired, there is almost always a heavy price to pay in rebellious, miserable and frustrated actors who have been effectively bullied and coerced into performances in which they do not believe, and the quality of the work over time may deteriorate rapidly.

Ensemble work prepares a group for the creative mindset. It relieves the company of status anxiety and leaves all their energies free for invention. Many of the games used to generate this state in a group are called trust exercises and many of them do depend on generating a sense of trust – a freedom from anxiety about how one will be received.

My grandmother's hat

The rules of communication, in this context of co-creation, are very simple: You say "Yes!" to whatever is given. Then you make an unembarrassed offer of whatever happens to occur to you, and that offer in turn is accepted and embellished. Importantly there is no plan. You both step off into the air and the solid ideas appear between you and your fellow actor, as if by magic. As you go on, they get clearer and stronger and you can both inhabit them for a time, responding easily to their internal logic.

But for the experience to be truly satisfying, at some stage early elements in the improvisation need to be recombined. This is what gives an improvisation a sense of direction and a hint of the narrative structure that we seem to need to make sense of the world. It also requires that from moment to moment you suspend your judgment and surrender your imagination to the offer that has been made. If you do not you are "blocking."

For example:

"That's a lovely green hat you are wearing ... "

"Thank you; it belonged to my grandmother ... "

As opposed to:

"That's a lovely green hat you are wearing ... "

"But I'm not wearing a hat ... "

Keith Johnstone explores this process in great detail in his classic book *Impro* (Johnstone 1979) which emerged from work he was doing at the Royal Court Theater back in the 1970s. It is an essential text. In it he describes many of the principles of improvisational technique that have become accepted practice. Some of these principles have their roots in the training of actors for the Commedia dell'Arte, the classic masked theater of the Italian Renaissance. In acting training this set of skills is core. Once learned, or perhaps re-remembered from childhood, they become second nature and the instinctive response to a suggestion becomes "Yes, and ... " This is the default state of actors when they are rehearsing. They are alternating between the rhetorical process of making offers and the co-creational process of accepting and inhabiting the offers that are made to them.

In order to do this, actors have to surrender control of the direction of the emerging narrative. This is extremely hard to do and rarely happens among adults, although it often occurs among children, particularly, I think, among girls. Everything in our education, and everything we strive for, in our attempt to assert ourselves in the world and get what we think we want, militates against this attitude of accepting. It feels vulnerable. We have "lost the initiative." We may be lowering ourselves in the social hierarchy, an action particularly threatening to boys and men, but unless we find a way to be accepting, we will be unable to co-create. We will be unable to build something together. If we are looking for consensus, or innovation, or novelty – if we want creativity – then an element of this behavior is essential.

In the context of a theater rehearsal, everyone (including the director, who is ostensibly in charge and in control) is flitting in and out of this place of "accepting" from moment to moment. And it is much more than merely "accepting" in the sense of tolerating another's point of view. What is demanded is an attempt wholly to abandon oneself to the offer and work with it regardless of its implications for any ideas or directions you may be formulating. This makes people extremely anxious and they will never do it unless they are operating within a group where there is a very high level of mutual trust.

It helps, therefore, to have a director who is outside the process, responsible for ensuring that the tolerance and trust are in place, and able to select from what emerges from the improvisers and shape it into a narrative – to be the one who is there to make sense of things. In an improvised performance, this selection is often done by the audience: either overtly, when they are asked to set constraints, or covertly, by the improvisers being sensitive and responding to the audience's reactions from moment to moment. In a rehearsal, the director is there in the role of audience and able to take the burden of responsibility for selecting from what is being created by the group who are improvising. The director can be trusted to hold the narrative.

Without a narrative, or the belief that someone knows what it is, we are afraid that we will not be able to make sense of events and we may discover that what we have been creating is nonsense. In an improvised show, for a paying audience, this may not matter too much. Nonsense often makes us laugh: at work, creating nonsense and being laughed at is our greatest fear. We do not necessarily need to be able to make sense of things ourselves, but we do need to believe that someone is watching us and that they are making sense of it. We can then suspend our own judgment, temporarily, about what is going on, and trust that at least it makes sense to someone. This is why we have, as a last resort, gods.

Improvisational conversations do occur among adults but are usually described as banter, or wise-cracking, or chatting. Both men and women spend much of their time having such conversations; indeed they are the social glue that binds communities (Tannen 1991). However, truly co-creational conversations are, in my experience, very rare in the context of work. There is something in the playfulness, in the lack of a clear direction and in the need for mutual surrender that almost defines improvisational conversation as outside the realm of "work." But for any creative emergence to happen these things are essential. Without them, work conversations are essentially adversarial or competitive, and tend to reduce the number of possible options and ideas, rather than increase them. When a group achieves the level of trust necessary for everyone to know that whatever they say will be accepted and welcomed then real creativity is possible. When this trust is in place it is possible for people to give voice to their first thoughts to let their half-baked, fragmentary, tentative ideas out into the open for consideration and perhaps completion by the other intelligences in the room.

The Three Fears

The competitive tradition, the idea of hierarchy and the anxiety we feel about relative status, inhibits us. It is a mindset profoundly ingrained and it stops creativity in its tracks. In his book, Keith Johnstone (1979) outlines the blocks to improvisation that inhibit us from this kind of process. I call them the Three Fears:

– Fear of being wrong.

– Fear of being rude.

– Fear of seeming mad.

And in most working environments these fears are deep. To appear offensive, insane and/or factually incorrect could safely be described as most employees' worst possible nightmare. So we keep our crazy ideas to ourselves and they remain half-baked, never getting out into the group where they might finish cooking.

One reason for this is obviously lack of time. Trust takes time to build, even with the help of the intensive games and exercises that are part of theater practice. Improvisations may mill about before they take off in a clear direction and rarely is there enough time allocated to allow this to happen. The absolute dominance of the idea of "efficiency" means that if conversations are not planned, structured or "facilitated" in some way then there is a danger of things degenerating into the much-feared "talking shop," where no outcomes can be recorded, and time has been wasted in "idle conversation."

This is indeed a danger, but only because groups left without constraints usually fall into unstructured competition, rather than co-creation, because people have not been trained to improvise together, and there is a fear, among some, of the sense of confusion and "being lost" that happens when you enter the infinitely complex boundary zone that is the essential transitional state between one stable proposition and an equally stable but completely novel one. Watercooler conversations are more likely to be co-creational because people are free to engage with those they trust and like, and are not in a group situation where the usual status games that dominate working life are operating.

As with most things in the arts, improvisation is a craft discipline. It has clear rules and principles, it requires endless practice to perfect technique, and it can be rigorously applied to produce specific and concrete results. From the point of view of the director of a creative process an understanding of this co-creational style is essential. Directors need to be masters both of the rhetorical, story-telling, pedagogical mode that is necessary for framing the constraints and selecting and fixing the useful ideas, and also of the co-creational mode where they can be alongside the actors, encouraging and helping them to develop the ideas they are trying to express. But perhaps the most important role in this respect is to establish the context of trust – to model, and to enforce, the rules of the community of trust within which the creative group is operating.

Suspending status games: the creative ensemble

So what is it like to be in group that does not play status? At the heart of good theater is the ensemble. In the European theater and increasingly in Britain this has come to mean a particular style or process for creating work. At its core is a team of people who are able to suspend their status games to devote all their attention to the task of creating the play.

A group of managers are sitting on the ground in a circle. They look uncomfortable and embarrassed.

"Here is the task. I want you all to close your eyes and then, as a group, count from one to thirty. I want to hear one voice at a time, if two of you speak at the same moment you must all start again at the beginning." They all close their eyes.

"One," says someone, a man in a neatly ironed shirt. "Two," says another. "Three!" – a man and a woman together.

"Start again."

"Why don't we just go round in a circle?"

"Because that's not the point – start again"

"One" The man in the ironed shirt starts the game again. "Two." A pause... "Three." Then "Four," a young man, very quickly, in a breathless, tight voice.

"Five." A long pause. The tension in the room is palpable. There is a fierce concentration, people straining to listen, their eyes squeezed shut, desperate to detect some hint that will allow them to know whether another in the group is about to speak or not. There is no sense to this, no plan, no order and no way of seeing the tiny nuances of expression that normally alert us to the subtle rules of "who speaks next." Some faces are tense with concentration, or maybe anger; they look irritated with the game and the group, their eyes screwed shut, their jaws clenched. On other faces there is a look of wry amusement, even delight. As the pauses lengthen, these people begin to grin widely, enjoying the excitement of the silence: "Who next? Not me!"

They reach fifteen before two people speak together and the game is stopped.

As soon as they open their eyes the man in the ironed shirt blurts out his exasperation. "We had an order going, it was you, you, then you and I was doing the second odd number, in that sequence." He is only half aware that this experience was unique to him. "I was just waiting for a space," says another. "It was like a meditation."

We try again. The concentration deepens. The group have been told to notice their reactions, to note their own response to the exercise and let it go. The game can only be completed when everyone is in the same relationship to the task. No one can drive it; no one can impel it. Everyone must only listen, and the space to speak will appear.

The game goes on; there is a gentle shift of energy. The group are concentrating just as hard, but there is less tension; people are relaxing, finding out how much energy you really need to listen. The voices become deeper, more confident. The numbers are spoken into the space with resonance and clarity. A curious rhythm emerges, the voices become measured. The pauses are longer, but are filled with a vibrant focused concentration, their silence intense. You can feel everyone reaching out into the silence trying to make contact. The group reaches thirty with no one interrupting and bursts into spontaneous applause.

In the work of many of the great ensemble directors they may spend half of the time available for completion of the finished performance in doing games and exercises to align the group. Working this way, where rehearsals routinely begin with structured explorations of how we connect, and find rapport, being there for others as much as for yourself becomes as natural as breathing. As the rehearsal process continues and favorite games emerge, the ensemble part can become merely a warmup. Exercises that took an hour three weeks ago are speeded through in minutes, a swift tuning up to the consciousness of others. Working in this way produces solidarity within the group that yields astonishing benefits for the creative process. It leads to the development of a rapport that allows for the simplest, most subtle gesture or germ of an idea to be explored.

A group with this training are often almost magical to watch. Ideas are developed without words, there seems to be an almost telepathic understanding between the actors and director. A nod or a grunt will be enough encouragement to allow an idea to be taken to its ends and thoroughly aired. It is this state to which a true ensemble strives – one where, at the forefront of everyone's conscious effort, there is the commitment to making the work well. Ideas are common property; suggestions emerge from anyone and are immediately explored and transcended.

The atmosphere is the diametric opposite of that in most of the business meetings I have been invited to facilitate. There, the air squeaks with tension; people are watchful, entrenched. Ideas are proposed in a spirit of conquest, lobbed into the space like mortars, and the proponent stands braced for attack as soon as her idea is launched. One major organization enshrines this attitude in the "duty to dissent" – a perverse kind of mechanism to ensure that no one gets swept along and nothing original or daring can take flight. Tentative ideas are therefore expounded with a kind of hysterical certainty – a desperate bid for ideological dominance at one fell swoop. Challenges are parried and "killer arguments" deployed to "blow the idea out of the water." Anything other than the most routine administrative matter is a battlefield. Nothing could be further from the passionate playfulness of the rehearsal, the open exploration and the frequent laughter that accompanies the witty or the unexpected turn of thought that ensemble work encourages.

Learning and practicing the disciplines of ensemble working are essential for generating creativity in a group. The payoffs are the possibility of innovation and passionate commitment from the group to the ideas generated. Ensemble disciplines are essential for a good rehearsal. Rehearsal is not the same as practicing. It is a creative act. It allows both for incremental improvements by repetition and also for co-creation – for the exploration and discovery of ideas. It also allows space for everyone in the group to make a contribution. In most organizations where there is a focus on speed and efficiency there is seldom an ensemble approach, and there is rarely time for rehearsal or an understanding of what a rehearsal is. There is a model of change that is patterned around the engineering metaphor of planning and implementation. Plans are drawn up and then implemented; there is no possibility of trying things out, of tinkering with the proposal in real time in order to emerge the best solution, like scientists and artists do in their labs and studios, and groups of actors in the rehearsal room.

All of the above locations have in common the idea of a safe space, usually scruffy and a bit battered, where mistakes can safely be made and failure celebrated for what it teaches rather than what it achieves. Making these spaces available within organizations is not common practice, and when they are made available the groups that go into them are not often trained in the disciplines of ensemble working, improvisation, rehearsal and co-creation. "Ideas" sessions are often just structured meetings in a different sort of room, with a few "wacky" exercises thrown in.

Ensemble working teaches people how to suspend the status games that undermine group creativity. They allow for the generation of a truly fertile environment for innovation. Rehearsal allows for the possibility of the genuinely unexpected and for every potential viewpoint to be expressed. This is essential because creativity is a boundary phenomenon. It comes about where different perspectives, different approaches, skills and beliefs meet. Innovation thrives where there is diversity (and potentially) conflict of opinion. Without diversity you will get creativity within the existing boundaries, you will tend to get variations on what is known and usual. If you have the potential both for diversity to be expressed and for challenge, you are more likely to get innovation, for the unexpected to emerge as well.

CHAPTER 8

Creativity, Innovation and Leadership

Men in tights and old music: the paradox of innovation in the arts

I love the ballet. It bores me for long stretches but then there is always a moment when the combination of the music and the story and the dancers' movements makes me weep when I least expect it. Some of the repertoire of classical ballet has been unchanged since the nineteenth century when much of the music was composed. Male dancers still wear tights, a style that went out of fashion in Europe in about 1560. There is a repertoire of movements that must be mastered by all classical dancers that has been pretty much unaltered for a hundred and fifty years. There is a paradox here: the arts seem to contain both unbroken lines of traditional practice and the ability to innovate and surprise. Of course great art endures because it still resonates. It connects with something unchanging in us, and so "old" art is still current and still in circulation, unlike old cars or old telephones. How do the arts, which at one level are steeped in craft and tradition, also become the source of radical and sometimes shocking innovation?

One could argue that, in Western European culture, no one made better or more beautiful pots than the ancient Greeks, no one painted better than the Renaissance painters. No one made better flint arrowheads than the late Stone Age. We look at these artifacts of craft tradition with awe. They are still, today, unsurpassed in their technical accomplishment. These productions were transcended not by mastery of the craft, but by technical innovation. So what causes the innovations? Where do they come from? How does innovation happen in the arts, given that so much of artistic production is within its own traditions rather than beyond them?

The answer is that innovation is provoked by contact with ideas outside your field of expertise. When the ironfounder and the barrelmaker meet the wagonbuilder and the mining engineer, you get the steam engine. It does not come from the inspiration of a single mind but the cross-fertilization of different craftsmen with different and finely advanced craft skills in their field. The early Modern movement in European painting was highly influenced by encounters with the work of African artists, the Impressionists by work in optics and breakthroughs in photography and the scientific understanding of light. The story of innovation is all too often told in terms of the narrative of the one with the visionary idea. But artistic (and scientific and technical innovation) is never the result of a sole genius working alone.

I spent a fascinating day in the studios of Anthony Gormley, the internationally renowned sculptor, watching him as he talked with the crew of fellow artists and craftspeople that made his works. The relationship was very close to the director and actor. Gormley had a vision for a work; had successfully communicated it to the people in his studio, but was responding in delight to the challenges and solutions they brought to him as they grappled with the technical problems of bringing that vision to life. It was so clearly a two-way process. Gormley understood, but did not possess, his team's skills in metalworking – but they clearly co-owned the problems of the technical constraints that his vision generated and there was a mutual passion about resolving them, together with a shared excitement about serendipitous discoveries that might suggest a new direction, a new form the work could take.

That fine artists – painters, sculptors – often work collaboratively with a team of people in their studio is not news, but it is little known outside the arts. The studios of all the great Renaissance masters were like this, and any great artist would be expected to have a coterie of apprentices, assistants and protégés that formed a working community. Few of the discoveries in the early days of the scientific enlightenment in the eighteenth century could have occurred without the craftsmen who blew the glass vessels and made the seals and the pipework and the balances which allowed for the experimental apparatus to be constructed. Often innovations in science were made by craftsmen. In fact it was only in 1833 that the word scientist was coined to make a distinction between the gentleman natural philosopher and the artisans who actually made experiments and experimental apparatus.

The solitary plagiarist

Innovation in the sciences or the arts is always as a result of masters of a craft meeting challenges suggested by contact with other masters outside their field of expertise. The innovator, the inventor, is often merely the one who, like the director, frames the constraints and urges the ensemble of talents connected with the project to bring forth a solution to the questions he or she has framed. Innovation emerges from dialog with other experts. Ideas may be born in individual reverie, but ideas are just stuff in your head; they are worthless until incarnated.

We have all been seduced by the idea of the solitary genius. The most vulnerable to this seduction have been the geniuses themselves. The title is too flattering to repudiate and the drive and ambition that goes with break-through thinking is often accompanied by a narcissistic personality that is oblivious to, or disparaging of, the contribution of others and the context in which their own ideas are generated. This problem is greatly exacer-bated by the contribution of a very important but often overlooked group, who have helped to create and to disseminate the idea of the solitary genius – the critics, commentators and historians who write the narratives of progress.

Artists are very seldom able to name the source of a specific idea or recall the influence that led them to it. Critics do this all the time and assume that the connections they notice from the outside are conscious choices made by the artist. This is very rarely the case. Artists plagiarize by accident rather than intent; as Jon Courtney Grimwood has noted:

> A fact from *New Scientist* or a snippet from that morning's news, a child seen crying in Caffè Nero or a boy stamping on his mobile on the corner of Oxford Street … Anything and everything is fair game. It's like bees chewing paper to make nests or birds stealing twigs; the worlds we create are constructed from bits of the world we inhabit.

> … All I can say in our defence is that it's entirely unintentional. Fragments and memories come together on the page in a way that seems, to the person writing, to be entirely new. (*The Guardian,* 27 August 2005)

Reading reviews of your own theater productions can be most enlightening – and sometimes bizarre: – to be told that you have cleverly revisited Peter Brook's production of 1972 when you thought you were doing a Sergio Leone remake, for example. This casual misattribution is rife and seldom challenged. Critics make assertions about the sources of things in art works but never seem to check back with the artist to see if that *was* actually how they came to make it that way. Artists seldom object because critics often assume a greater deliberating intelligence at work in the art than is actually the case. Often the artistic process feels more like just fiddling with it till it seems to come right. The critic's view is too flattering to be gainsaid.

One of the things that obsesses businesses for obvious reasons but is actually not very high on the artist's list of concerns is what the customers or audience think. There is little or no direct consultation with the audience about how an artwork should be, in the same way that "pure" scientists are little concerned with the utility of their discoveries in layperson's terms. The conversations artists have tend more to be with the field of other artists. Artists are a community of experts, like physicists, and therefore they are only going to have their mind exercised by dialog with other experts. In the case of art some of these dialogs are with the works, rather than the people who make the works, but the principle is very much the same. Books are made from other books – so of painting, music and ballet.

Artists feel the need to push out the boundaries of convention only when they've exhausted the conventions that exist, and the spur to this effort is often provoked by competition with, or admiration for, the work of another artist. Artists come at the boundaries of their field from the inside, as it were – from a situation of being immersed in the practice. This is a product of the unique problems connected with the teaching and dissemination of artistic skills. The arts operate a master–apprentice model of pedagogy which is the only way of successfully transmitting the embodied rather than intellectual skills that are the defining characteristic of the arts. These craft conventions are important not because they are a restraint but because they are part of the soup of ideas out of which further ideas grow (of which more later). Innovation in the arts is often framed in terms of a dialog with tradition or existing practice. The arts do not abandon the old in pursuit of the new. Artists begin to innovate only when they have reached the limits of their craft and begun to transgress the boundaries.

Creativity and innovation are therefore heavily contextualized. Art is made from other things; ideas are made from other ideas; they are not the product of lonely geniuses and blank paper. There is no creativity without context. Solitude and reflection are essential parts of the process, but people who make things and innovate, whether these innovations are works of art, steam engines, theories, or suspension bridges, are always working from within a community of others; other people, other ideas, other crafts and practices. Half of the business of generating innovation lies in noticing, bringing together and managing these communities – and who exactly is in these communities matters a lot.

Casting and diversity: the concentric organization

Businesses often use an organizational tree to express their structure. These old genealogies show the hierarchy of the organization with the boss at the top and then down through the ranks of power and wealth to the drones and doers at the bottom. These pictures tell a part of the organizational story but bring with them a lot of unhelpful baggage about hierarchies and ascent and descent, rank and position, and so on. Theater companies, and to an extent other organizations that have a "theater" at their heart (like the army or a hospital) really have a concentric structure, more like an onion than a tree. At the heart of the organization is the theater where the defining activity of the organization goes on – the stage, the theater of war, the operating theater and the rest of the organization is layered around it.

In there, at the symbolic and practical heart of the organization, are a cast of characters playing a variety of different roles, of greater or lesser importance but all vital to a successful outcome. Very close around the core actors is the next layer of the onion, people whose roles are intimately and personally connected with the central drama of the organization but who may not be actually be "on stage." Around them comes another layer of support, often more physically removed from the location of the action, and so on outwards and in most cases upwards (in terms of rank and salary) to the outermost and most distant ring or layer.

In organizations like this, there are two hierarchies operating: that of management structure and pay and that of closeness to the action. Concentric organizations tend to revere those closest to the action, and people are more likely to be passionate and committed to their work if they are close to it, however humble their position in the organizational tree. The further away they are from the "theater of operations," the more marginal they are likely to feel.

Even if they are ostensibly more important in the organizational tree, they will often struggle to achieve the status, respect and recognition within the organization that someone more lowly but closer in to the action might get. They will struggle to be accepted and quickly become "them."

There was a dresser at the Royal Shakespeare Company, for example, called "Black Mac" who became quite a well-known and influential "character" in the backstage community, despite his position almost at the bottom of the organizational tree. People like this in an organization may be better known, and their views more influential, than those of the financial director, in terms of the day-to-day gossip of organizational life, because of their intimacy with the key players, their closeness to the core, defining activity, of the organization.

The same is true in a hospital and the army; mess servants, batmen and hospital porters are important players in the organizational drama for those close to the action. This fact of life is amply illustrated in Shakespeare's plays. He always gives time and space to the lower ranks, the servants and pot-boys, the ostlers and footsoldiers, because in Elizabethan communities, built around the fundamental organizing unit of the "household," these characters were important – and not just functionally, in keeping people fed and watered, but also in supporting or undermining the social context in which the power-wielding characters are attempting to achieve their objectives; and often having small but vital roles to play in facilitating or thwarting the grand schemes of power.

When I am invited to strategy meetings or awaydays with organizations, these characters are never there. They are not invited; and their contribution is assumed or ignored, or occasionally guessed at, but never properly represented. For me, too many "teambuilding" or "strategy" days are the equivalents of being asked to direct *Hamlet* and turning up to find a room full of twenty young male actors, all desperate to play the lead. If you are rehearsing *Hamlet*, you need to have all the people there who are involved in telling the story, even if their only job is to run in with a letter at just the right moment. At some stage, if only briefly, you need to have them there to rehearse.

There are two very good reasons for this. One is that the thing may not work otherwise, and the second is that they will have information, tacit knowledge and a perspective on the whole project that might just provide the germ of a transformational intervention that will change things. By not having them represented you are depriving yourself, as director, of potentially vital creative resources.

You can of course rehearse *Hamlet* with a room full of Hamlets; they can have a guess at Gertrude's motivations, and they can roughly imagine the other parts and do them more or less well. They might produce a very interesting version of the play, in fact, but they would have a lot of trouble if they then went to a talented, middle-aged actress of some experience and said "We've rehearsed this role for you and we want you to do it like this ... " This is possible of course, but not remotely as successful or interesting a process as actually having that player in the room and having her fully participate in the rehearsals.

What play are we in?

People can't really handle a group of more than about twenty-five and keep charge. In reality, groups larger than this fragment and power is delegated to, or taken by, subgroup leaders. Creativity in complex organizations where there are a large number of individuals involved needs to reflect that diversity in order to generate initiatives that will be readily understood and enacted by the organization. Diversity also greatly increases the possibility of boundary-transgressing innovations. The ensemble model of group creativity under the leadership of a creative director is a good enough model for bringing that about.

If you look at the structure of an organization with a heart, like the army or the theater, or the medical profession, it tends to organize around a central cast of characters who really matter and who make the organization's impact on the world. These ensembles are never very large. There seems to be a functional limit to the size of highly motivated, mobile and creative teams that lies around 25 individuals. In practice all of us, in all aspects of our lives, can describe interlocking sets of groups that are the functional units of our lives as social animals.

We have parts to play in many of these groups. I have a role as a parent at my daughter's school; as a participant in various working parties and alliances to which I contribute as a teacher in a university; as a consultant in business; or as a member of my non-work friendship group. Throughout my working life I have been active in many of these functional teams but they have rarely matched the conventional structures that they have impacted on.

I also have very different-sized parts to play in each one of them. I have a starring role as "Dad" in the play entitled "My Family's Life." I have a much smaller but still important role as "Father at the School Gates" in the play entitled "My Life at School" starring my daughter. These two plays interlock – I appear in both. But I will make a grave error if I think I am the star of my daughter's play. I need to think very carefully about how I play that "Father at the School Gates" part. It is only a walk-on role but it can have a devastating impact on the play and the performance of my daughter (who *is* the star of that production) if I get it wrong, or forget what that play is actually about. This is really easy to do. We like to think of ourselves as consistent, as whole and authentic. We do not like to think that we "act different" with different people. We think of this as false and artificial behavior. But this (relatively modern) obsession with psychological integrity can blind us completely to the impact we have on others and the success of our performance in facilitating the success of the whole ensemble.

It can be a very valuable exercise to think in terms of the repertoire of performances you are obliged to give in life and think more deeply about who are the protagonists and who the supporting players, who really matters to the unfolding of that story through time. Who are the cast of the creative ensemble who animate that project? How is it best to play your role and, more interestingly, when do you get to rehearse and who do you get to direct those rehearsals?

It is difficult for me to convince organizations that most of their strategy days and teambuilding sessions are a waste of time because they do not

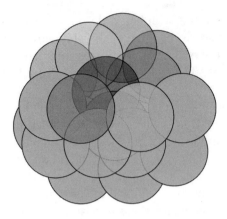

Life looks more like this than the traditional picture below; with people making appearances in a number of different spheres many of which overlap, playing roles of differing size and importance.

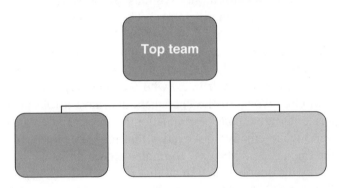

Figure 8.1 Concentric and hierarchical organizational diagrams.

have the right cast in the room. There seems to be a belief that if people are in the same building, or in the same type of job, or at the same level in the organization, that they must be some kind of team (see Figure 8.1). This is rarely the case and very rarely would they represent what a theater director would recognize as a cast. The cast are the actors in the play, the people you need to tell the story. But very few organizations think in story terms.

Stars and bit-players

In any play there are, essentially, protagonists and bit-players. Protagonists can be described roughly as characters who move the story on, while bit-players provide the context and sometimes the crucial links and bits of information that make the story hang together. You can cut a Shakespeare play down and perform it with half a dozen actors but you will still need some of those bit-parts to be there or the play will not work. Minor characters provide vital perspectives. They may only have one line in a whole play, but if the line is "The queen, my lord, is dead," the play will not work without them.

Rehearsal is not just practicing and it is not about the director telling the actors what to do. It is about co-creation. Under the eye of the director and operating within the constraints set by the director, the cast of characters experiment and play around with all the infinitely varied and nuanced ways in which they can, as a team, enact the performances required of them and agree the most powerful and effective option.

Many of these elements are there in business meetings. The director or directors are there. Some of the protagonists are there, but not the others. The constraints are known, although these always seem to me to be exactly the same, whatever the organization: "We must grow by 10 to 15 per cent in the next 12 months while cutting costs." The core activity of the organization is known, but always most of the vital players are missing; the van drivers, the head of finance, the admin support staff, a shareholder, the call center staff, the PA, the field engineer. They need to be represented by someone who knows their lines, who sees the play entirely from their perspective. Only when all the characters that have a role in the part of the corporate narrative under examination are represented can you really rehearse and make creative discoveries that may transform the organization on the one hand and be easy to implement on the other, because they were made by the people who will do that role.

It is hard enough to get a young drama school student to be relaxed and confident enough to do good work with a leading star actor. It is even harder to create (quickly) the conditions within which the head of finance for the area health authority (say) can work productively with a part-time, contract cleaner to rehearse the successful, long-running show entitled "Hospital Toilets Are Spotlessly Clean!" which urgently needs to be playing nightly at a hospital near you. But it can be done.

Too many Hamlets

Within many of the senior management "teams" in organizations, there is still a terrible lack of diversity. It is not necessarily that the organization is not diverse, but senior managers are still, in many sectors of industry, homogenous groups composed of very few women and lots of 30-to-55-year-old males with similar social and educational backgrounds. This produces a particular micro-culture, which quickly pushes people towards an even narrower permitted range of behavior. The degree of diversity in my experience differs markedly from sector to sector but there is still a dominance of white males in heavy industry and engineering, although there is more diversity in the creative and service sectors.

The problem is not only that there is still a dominance of white men in senior management but that the groups they inhabit are brought together to solve problems on behalf of the whole organization – an organization which is often far more diverse than is reflected in the senior management cadre. Even in organizations where there is diversity, at board or partner level, where the story of the organization is written and rehearsed, there are no bit-players, no walk-on parts, no one to represent the telling detail of the organization's operations from an informed perspective. Not only are these groups relatively homogenous in age and cultural background; they are almost always working within the same or equivalent place in the organizational hierarchy.

This may not strike anyone in an organization as odd, but if the group are to do creative work then it is a big problem. It is exactly like trying to put on a production of *Hamlet* with a room full of Hamlets. They cannot bring to their deliberations the felt experience of other worlds that a well-cast group of actors can. They do not represent, in their diverse perspectives, the tacit knowledge of the activities and worlds that exist in the organization they are being brought together to work on. And most important they do not have the ability to bring the telling detail to the rehearsal process.

Fake creativity

In the usual rush of getting things done there is a demand for precision and clarity, and management has become better and better at ensuring this kind of clarity is in place. But there has been a heavy price in terms of the space to go deeper, and, more important, to maintain contact with the bigger, more complex currents that will provide the emerging new directions as an organization evolves or as circumstances change.

Exploring this deeper territory in a systematic way is what the arts do. If there is one big difference between business processes and creative processes, it is that in business people proceed to implementation too soon. All ideas start off half-baked. In a creative process you look for a hundred of them before you begin to cook any. In business, all too often, the guilt attached to considering, thinking, mulling and meditating (which don't get into the basket labeled "work;" in fact these skills are often labeled "procrastination" or, worse, "indecisiveness") means that the first half-baked idea that gets consensus gets implemented with great efficiency and then has to be redesigned, adapted, withdrawn or lived with when it turns out to be no good or has negative unforeseen consequences.

Part of this is due to the fact that the processes for managing group creativity are not well understood. Imagining and mulling as a group activity are not done efficiently. The model for group creative processes in most organizations (as much as it exists) is death by flipchart. Go to a hotel for two days, get drunk, argue, draw diagrams, and go home. The conversations on these awaydays, the ones that happen in between the scheduled events, are sometimes useful, but our model for important conversations is often not a good one. It is usually based on the school debate. This process is supposed to be "democratic" and therefore good. It would be democratic if organizations took votes of all their stakeholders on the outcomes of "discussions," but they don't. So what you are left with is the competitive debating of a parliament or a law court in which ideas are pitched against each other in an adversarial contest.

Even in the best of these sorts of meetings the victorious suggestions are then appropriated, adapted or ignored by the powerful, according to other agenda, that are seldom explicit at the meeting. This is not a creative process: it is a competitive, reductive one. It is a model for quickly reducing the numbers of ideas in the room to one – and usually the one that fits with the predetermined objectives of the most senior people present. Another trouble with debating rituals is that they oblige the participants to deny or disguise the fact that their ideas are half-baked. Most ideas are half-baked; they need to be developed and changed and in a group situation some of this work needs to be done collaboratively. The debate is not good at this. If you are in an essentially competitive conversational space, you will find yourself very quickly defending the indefensible, or at least making bigger claims for a fragmentary idea than is wise.

CHAPTER 9

Live Communication: The Business of Theater

Acting training begins with the body. Our bodies provide the context of everything we say, and as animals we are vastly more sensitive and responsive to physical signals than we are to the meanings of words. Ape groups have complex social hierarchies; they may even be capable of understanding complex language. They can be taught to communicate extremely sophisticated ideas using standard sign language. But the majority of what they communicate is by actions and a limited range of grunts. This does not make them unsophisticated socially. Power play, love, friendship, alienation, bullying, altruism – all these behaviors and more are observed and recorded among ape communities. It is almost impossible for people who work closely with them not to see them as almost human. But this obscures the truth. Apes are not like us in some surprising ways. We are almost exactly like them. The extraordinary sophistication of human language blinds us to the fact that for the most part we hardly use it. We may be able to express our ideas with great subtlety and clarity using language, but the content of what we say to someone rarely lands without most of its meaning lost or corrupted on the way. The bulk of what actually gets communicated successfully between people in a face-to-face communication is signed and signaled by body language and intonation, as it is with other apes.

The difference between a transcript of a real conversation and a section of dialog from a play is huge. Even the most naturalistic-sounding dialog in a play is highly crafted and artificial. In films, dialog may be almost completely absent. The opening titles of many films can be masterpieces of storytelling entirely without words. We watch the actions and expressions of the characters skillfully filmed and cut together and in a few minutes of film, without a word spoken, we know who they are, what they are like, what they do, sometimes who they love and who they fear. This visual and contextual communication, the visual and the visceral, is most of what we receive and recall from interaction with others. The content of their speech and the meaning of what they say comes way behind.

And, worryingly, we are increasingly moving back towards a non-verbal culture. We are getting closer to our ape cousins; we are getting less and less able to decode the spoken word and less adept at using it. The visual has always dominated and this domination is becoming a tyranny. We are less good at listening and less good at telling stories. One hundred and fifty years ago people would ride all day to stand and listen to a four-hour sermon. Keeping an audience's attention through a four-hour play is nearly impossible despite all the technical wizardry of today's theater. Ironically, this seems to have made us more susceptible to stories rather than less. We are more easily swayed by a good story and a few images. We do not listen in detail. This is great for advertising and politics but very danger-ous for everything else, particularly when it comes to situations where the detail matters.

Being self-conscious

The big stage of a traditional theater is a machine for amplifying the human soul. As soon as you set foot on the empty space and are regarded, you will be revealed. What matters most in a live performance is how you are when you say something and the context in which you say it. So train-ing begins with the body, by becoming aware of your physical state.

One of the simplest, and hardest, early exercises is to come on stage and do nothing.

"Just walk across the stage – do nothing."

I did.

"No, not like that!" he said. "Do nothing!"

I tried again, consciously relaxing and trying to look neutral (but charismatic).

"No, no, no! Stop flirting! Just walk."

I tried again, my mind as empty as possible and my body relaxed.

I got to the other side.

"You need to do some work on that," he said. "You walk like a duck."

So I did ballet, physical training, Alexander technique, movement class, clown and mask work, acrobatics. Over the years, I gradually gained more conscious control of the signals I give off. I still walk like a duck, but a much more relaxed and charismatic one.

Most of the response you get from the audience will be provoked by these physical signals. When you see an actor stroll onto the stage to slump down in a sunny room, you are watching a piece of enormously subtle acrobatics. If you see an actress fumbling for a cigarette, it is arti-fice, the result of highly trained consciousness, not only about her own body but, more important, about exactly what she needs to do to provoke the response she wants in you.

We are sensitive to these signals at a microscopic level. We can instantly sense when someone we are with makes us uneasy or flustered, or angry, or bored – we may not be conscious of what exactly has made that feeling come, but it will be there and will affect us. We are responding and adjusting to this context all the time. Most of our brain has developed in order to process these signals that are so crucial to us as social animals. But we are generally unconscious of it; we tend to live in our own thoughts and constantly rationalize and invent a continuity that explains our responses. The more we do this the more likely we are to misread the signals or overreact to the feelings they provoke. In general people are not consciously aware that this context is being generated or how. They are subject to an emotional context that colors the quality of the communication and can easily override the rational content of what is being said.

A simple example is the deadly process of feedback or appraisal. Whatever is said in an appraisal, people will recall the negative before the positive. If the context is neutral they select the bad. People will only take a clear message if it is not neutral. They will respond to undiluted praise or to a harangue, but if there is very little emotional context they will make one, from the little signals they pick up and from the clamor of their own needs. It is tragically easy to be misled.

So step one in clarifying and developing the ability to communicate is to become aware of the body and the signals we give off.

Words and actions

The relationship between the content of what someone says and the intention behind the words is rich ground for confusion, manipulation, deceit or passionate truthfulness. Marrying the thought, the action and the words together is one the highest crafts of acting. As Hamlet advises the Player King: "Suit the action to the word, the word to the action, with this special observance, that you overstep not the modesty of nature."

Everything we say in a live communication is mediated by our bodies. Shakespeare was probably talking about gestures when he referred to "the action" in the quote above. In the Elizabethan theater, and for a long time afterwards, there was a highly sophisticated and formal code of gestures for every feeling and emotion. Some of these are recorded in later manuals of acting. They became highly stylized and persisted well into the nineteenth century. Despite Shakespeare's exhortation not to overstep the modesty of nature, things were looking very unnatural by the time the revolution in theater that led to contemporary naturalism began, towards the latter part of the nineteenth century.

We now pay very little attention to our bodies when we speak in public, or even in private. And yet most of what we receive and recall from a face-to-face communication is impression, not content, and these impressions are communicated by our bodies, not the meaning of our words.

One of the most important of these physical signals is the quality of eye contact. It is fascinating how powerful and how subtle this communication is. Not only is there variation between individuals in how they use eye contact; it is also highly culturally specific, a fact that is becoming more obvious as migration and globalization present us with more and more experience of other cultural norms.

The difficulty for most people when presenting to a live audience is that they are unprepared for the extraordinary effect of the human gaze. When someone stands up in a group of seated people they attract attention. This is almost instinctive. As soon as an individual stands higher than the group, the group will look at them. Any troupe of apes sitting in the forest will always look up to see, if one of their number stands up. They are likely to have something important to communicate. They are going to display for status or for sex or for fun, or they are going to warn the group of danger. Everyone instinctively pays attention. This attention lands on the speaker with a surprising force. There is a surge of adrenaline and the longer you stand in front of an audience the higher this expectation builds in both of you until it can become almost unbearable. The desire to run away or fight builds up. You need to do something to justify the attention.

The secret is to be able to field this surge of emotions and the accompanying rush of adrenaline, and surf it. To keep your body relaxed and easy and expressive, whatever your adrenal glands are telling it to do. Most of the training of actors begins with making them self-conscious, literally conscious of all the physical stuff of which we are normally unconscious. The breath, how it comes in and out, the body, the tilt of the spine, the exact degree of tension or relaxation in every muscle, the tilt and intensity of the gaze, the degree of contact with the other actor or the audience. This physical training is exhaustive and rigorous, but when it is mastered it sets people free. They are able to let go of their habitual physicality and adopt whatever will support the needs of the moment. They also, for stage work, need gradually to develop a keen knowledge of the effects of what they do and how they hold themselves. This is harder to achieve.

In the end it becomes possible for an actor to stand in front of an audience and look totally relaxed and in command, and, eventually, sometimes, but not always, to feel that way too, to become unselfconscious in front of an audience – to lose the tension and anxiety that being looked at seems, for some reason, instinctively to provoke; it becomes possible to display whatever signals the audience need to receive to understand the feelings and the context of the performance. The same process is followed for the voice, in what is perhaps an even more intimate journey of training, self-knowledge and discovery. Having gone on this journey, actors then become rather odd people. It is as if this development ploughs up and releases whole areas of the personality that in most people are fallow. It is tied up with the problem of authenticity.

Many of the people I coach for public speaking who are not actors have a very strong and distinctive physicality. They have evolved through life into the shape they are. Their bodies and voices are distinctive, unique, quirky, and, sometimes, purely by chance, they will have evolved physical and vocal habits that give a strong signal to an audience. They may, for whatever reason, habitually tilt their head back a little when they speak and tend to look and sound just a little arrogant. They may have got into the habit of evading eye contact. As people get older they evolve a physical personality that sometimes can severely inhibit or distort the context of their communications.

But people perceive this carapace as being intimately connected with "who they are." It is as if this set of physical quirks and mannerisms were an intimate part of their personality. It certainly must feel that way, and the work of shifting these characteristics in people who emphatically have no desire to "act" can be a delicate task. But for me as an actor it raises very interesting questions. Having been through the experience of having my voice and body trained (although my own professional training was sporadic, and far less rigorous than some) I can see that I both still have my own, very distinctive physicality, yet I am free of it. This is quite useful and no threat to my sense of self. I have gained from this craft the possibility of communicating a wider range of thoughts and feelings with more power than I could before, and a subtly different view of what really constitutes me, the person I am. It is as if acting training makes more of you available to others and the core self actually shrinks. Actors in fact have a rather small ego; that is why they are so sensitive.

This ability to make more of oneself available to others is also core to the skills of "reacting." Or more accurately of listening, receiving and responding to what you are being given by the other actors. This is the heart of the skill of improvisation; a training that develops the ability to "say yes": to take in and go along with what is being offered, to let go of the desire to defend and assert yourself in the face of someone "acting" on you. It is the core behavior of co-creation; without it rehearsal is impossible, and creativity is stopped in its tracks.

The usefulness of Chinese whispers

Communication is one of the things that actors are supposed to be good at. What is clear to actors and less clear to others is that communication is primarily a physical skill rather than an intellectual one. The content that we are trying to communicate is always mediated by our physical self and by the presence of others. Even when we write, we use a voice that is distinctive to us and resonates very differently in our heads from how it is recreated in the heads of readers. In the end we co-create meaning; communication happens in the space between the actor and the audience and neither party has final control over what that meaning is.

Communication is crucial, but there are two big problems: one is the "what" and the other is the "how." The craft of acting is invaluable in helping with the how. The "what" is more difficult and becoming ever more so. This is not just because of the dramatic transformation of methods of communication brought by the technology revolution from email to video conferencing, from PowerPoint to mobile phones, but because increasingly organizations are dependent on, and very often produce, only ideas and propositions. The stuff companies trade in the world today is very often intangible and how it is communicated matters desperately.

The project of theater, and of any live communication, is to get people to converge in their understanding. You want people to understand what you say in the way that you understand it. This is, of course, impossible. The inside of each person's head is unique, and stuff will land in there in different ways whatever you do. People recall what they are interested in and they shape what they hear and what they see to fit with the world-picture they have grown through their life. Of course we can and do succeed in making people agree that they have shared the same experience as us. But we should know that this shared understanding might be quite fragile. This fragility is easily shown in a modified version of the children's party-game that used to be called "Chinese whispers."

In the original children's game, one person whispers a message, very quietly, to the next in a line who then passes it on to another and so on. through several iterations, until the last person in the line says the message out loud. Sometimes the message has changed in an amusing way. There are two other versions of this game that, despite their simplicity, yield some interesting insights into successful communication.

The first version is "physical Chinese whispers." It works best with a group of at least ten. Half of the group leave the room and one person is invited to sit on a chair in a striking and slightly distorted pose. For the game to work, you must be able to reproduce the pose exactly at the end of the exercise, so you need to set it up with care. Then you invite the other participants in, one by one and each one is given ten seconds to observe the pose in as much detail as possible and is then invited to reproduce the pose by taking the place of the person in the chair.

One by one the people come in, examine the pose and then replace the person in the chair, trying to sit exactly as they were sitting. Of course there are "errors in copying" between the individuals and the final pose ends up looking quite different from the first one. But the game provokes laughter in the audience, as the group watching see each participant building on the "error" of the last one. The person who comes in two or three down the line to mimic the pose cannot tell which bit of the pose is original and which bit is an accretion.

Curiously, when you are playing the game, this never occurs to you. As a player, you are focused intently on observing and trying to absorb as much information as you can, as accurately as you can, to achieve the task. Not only is it impossible to tell which bit of the pose is original, but somehow it does not occur to you to ask this question; the pose is the pose. You accept what is in front of you as "the truth;" you are preoccupied with trying to understand it as fully and as quickly as you can.

As a member of the audience, watching the series of iterations unfold before you, a strange phenomenon sometimes occurs. If you get a group to do seven or eight iterations, the audience see a kind of story emerging. An open hand gesture will become exaggerated into a wave. A crossed leg will become an extravagant lolling of the whole limb. A fixed gaze will gradually morph into a worried frown as people notice and unconsciously embellish a detail, in a search for meaning that they can use to help them with the task. Watching from the audience, you see the pose go on a journey. It develops a mood; sometimes it becomes something subtly and strikingly different.

What is happening here is not merely "error" in copying but creative emergence. The mere fact of someone trying to receive a communication and then express it again, clearly, to another is a complex enough process for spontaneous creative emergence, for evolution, to occur. Even when people are intent on being true to the communication, when they are actively trying to be consistent, not creative, each person participating in the game receives the information contained in the pose in a way that is unique to them, and expresses it in a way that is unique to them, but also "makes sense" to them. The combined effect of this effort over several iterations generates another narrative that only the audience watching from the side can see. At the end of the game, with the last person sitting in the chair, the first person comes back and takes up the original pose.

This makes clear to the players what the audience have seen, and they are tempted to ask: "How did we get to that, when we were all trying our best to be clear?"

The same process occurs with a piece of text in the other version of the exercise. A short story from a newspaper is read to the first participant and each person entering the room is encouraged first to listen and then repeat the story as accurately as they can to the next participant; the same creative emergence occurs. People do not "mis-hear," as in the traditional party game of Chinese whispers; they unconsciously select from what they have heard. Different people find different bits of the communication "sticky," and over a series of iterations the story transforms into something else. Pieces of information are lost, new pieces are created from fragments of the other people's iterations, but the story holds together and always has a family resemblance to the original.

This simple exercise is a great introduction to the central problem of live communication. Whether it is a formal presentation, giving instructions to someone, or an informal conversation, the sense we are making of what we hear and how what we say is received, allows for the kind of "errors in copying" that are the raw material for creative evolution. You could say that the craft of theater is about minimizing this phenomenon in performance and exploiting it in rehearsal. We allow for creative emergence when we are making the communication event and then minimize it when we want to make the communication land on the audience in a specific way for a specific result.

Communication styles

You can look at this as a two different styles of communication (see Figure 9.1). The first is a style that is appropriate for co-creation and improvisation, a style that actively encourages and exploits the co-creational emergent space. The other is a style that is the opposite, what you could call a directive or rhetorical style, that uses technique to ensure consistency and clarity of a message – a communication style that tries to ensure that the communication lands in the same way on all the audience at the same time, so that they can have the same experience in the same way.

But beyond these broad emotional communal moments, things get difficult. People may agree that a particular moment in a play moved them to tears but they may have diverging explanations for why. In art this doesn't matter so much, and a whole industry of criticism and review is based on the enjoyable analysis of why it made people think or feel that way, but in business very often there is perceived to be a need for clarity

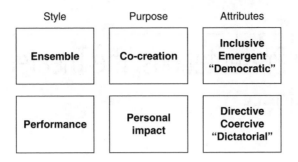

Figure 9.1 Communication styles and their uses.

and universality. Everyone needs to know and understand the same things about what is required of them – for due diligence in the eyes of the law, for example.

The recent incidence in big organizations of shocking lapses in this most important area makes it clear that communicating even these essential and unarguable basics is fraught with difficulty. If people cannot even grasp what is borderline illegal behavior, how can they be aligned around something as woolly and ambiguous as a mission statement?

CHAPTER 10

Giving Presentations: The Theater of Business

A group of managers are assembling for a strategy meeting in a Midlands hotel. The meeting starts at 1.00pm; many have driven from the far ends of the country to be there. They have lunch in the hotel restaurant and assemble in the conference suite. The room has a low white ceiling and a thick carpet. The light is very bright. The tables are laid out as for a wedding feast with a top table and two side tables but there is no food. Only water ...

In front of the tables, where, if this were a wedding feast, the dancing would be, there are various pieces of machinery. There is a TV monitor on a high mobile stand, a blank white screen, a video projector, a low stack of amplifiers, and computer equipment and DVD players. The whole assemblage, with its tangle of wires and blinking lights, makes the room look like an intensive-care ward in a hospital. Some hi-tech surgical intervention is going to take place and the senior regional manager is going to inflict it on his "team." By twenty past one the senior manager is halfway through his presentation. The room is warm, the voice drones on, sleep beckons ...

Theater people know that impact on the audience results from delivering an engaging and compelling event. The elements of this event include the content, the narrative, the message of the text, the moral, the cast, the setting, the costumes, the design, the venue: all the context of the interaction.

People will take away a perception of a live event that will include only a tiny part of the text that the event is based on. People can rarely recall the text of a performance of Hamlet, but they will recount the gist of the narrative, and report the impact. These are the elements of the interaction that will stay with them and inform their behavior and understanding after the performance. Business presentations are live events. In preparing a live event, attention needs to be given to all of the context of the interaction to reinforce and guide the audience's attention.

The problem with presentations is that they tend to be very content-focused. The text of a presentation is usually composed of facts and information. People do not readily engage with facts. They engage with narrative and emotion. If your desire is for people to take some action as a result of your presentation, if you want it to stay with them after the event, then some element of narrative and some engagement with emotion needs to be included in the communication. Narrative and emotion help to make a communication "sticky." So also do imagery and concrete detail. The text may contain information that is of interest to the audience, but the text should be viewed only as the framework on which the communication event is built.

However clear and well ordered your argument, however exciting and relevant the text, you are faced, in a live event, with a practical, physical problem. There is a gap between you and the audience. The craft of theater is to bridge that gap in a way that ensures the audience are compelled to listen and is riveted by the narrative unfolding before it. It is also usually desirable to achieve convergence of understanding: we want everyone to leave inspired by essentially the same ideas. The problem is that as soon as someone stands up in front of a group of people who are seated, a different dynamic enters the space. People will give you their attention; they will look and watch, expecting something. The power of this simple phenomenon is so overwhelming that most people find it deeply uncomfortable.

Bridging the gap

When someone speaks you receive what they are saying in many ways. Not only are the pace, intonation and power of their voice important but also the animation and engagement of their body, the setting, the light, the way they are dressed. These things together cause an emotional response in us that is very strong. Our engagement with the content of what someone is saying is always enmeshed with our total emotional response to them. If the person makes us feel anxious or irritated, no matter how compelling the content, our reaction to that content will be colored by these emotions. If they are not engaging with us directly, if we cannot see or hear them clearly, we will feel bored and detached; they will not be bridging the gap in space between us.

These responses are very deep-seated. They may reflect our relationship with apes of other kinds. Troops of apes sitting around in the forest need to give their attention to anyone who stands up and starts to bellow. It may be warning, or a mating display, or a bid for higher status in the group that everyone needs to be aware of. Whatever the origins of the response, there is no denying its physical power. The person who stands up in a circle of colleagues gets their attention in a way that causes the speaker to have an adrenaline rush. The exposure of their whole body to examination is enough of a trigger to get the audience aroused and interested at a very deep, unconscious level. It feels quite different when everyone in a group is sitting in a circle with their heads and bodies more or less in the same position. In that configuration it is much easier for anyone to speak.

Whatever the cause, there are two requirements for the actor to be able to handle the situation. First, they must cope with the adrenaline rush and not pick a fight or flee, and then they must use the attention they have been given to land their message on the audience in a way that the audience will get.

But of course you must land more than the words. As an actor, you need to do something to them. Acting is action. It is transitive; you are always trying to do something *to* someone, directly to the audience or indirectly by doing something to your fellow actors. You are always trying to "move them" to "take them with you." When a performance is going well, you feel as if "you are holding them in the palm of your hand." These metaphors of are apt. At its simplest level this is the ultimate task of live performance: to take the audience with you on an emotional and imaginative journey which will lead to a shared understanding.

Acting on – acting out: live communication as action

Actors and directors often use the idea of actions to animate the text they are working on. This can be done very systematically using transitive verbs to describe the action that goes with every line or thought of the text being spoken.

Transitive verbs are those that describe an action that can be done to an object. "To laugh" is a verb but it is not transitive: I cannot "laugh" someone. "To delight," or "to surprise," *is* transitive, however: I can delight someone or surprise them and they may laugh. Lists of transitive verbs are handy crib sheets for actors. Acting is action. That is all it is: acting on someone, acting on the audience, on your fellow actor. It is a wholly outward process, not an inward one. So that even when the words are all set down by the author, there is still space for the actor to interpret and change the impact of the moment in a subtle way, by examining different possible actions within the words.

If you take the line, "I'm going to kill you," its impact on the other actor or on the audience will change dramatically depending on the action you choose to play: the line will have a very different effect if the action is "to charm," "to tease" or "to seduce" from the effect if the action is "to terrify."

Actors continually ask the question, "What am I trying to do to them with what I am saying?" "They" may be the audience, or the partner in a dialog. Interestingly, depending on the context and the broader strategic aims of the actor within the scene (what is sometimes called "the super-objective"), you may successfully terrify the other actor by playing "to charm" or "to seduce" when the line contains a threat. This is called playing against the text. Hollywood baddies do it all the time.

Summary

There are three things that will always help a presentation make an impact:

– *Narrative*. If the content has some sort of narrative structure it will drive the presentation forward with energy; it will dramatize it. Drama needs a protagonist and antagonist; it needs to deal in conflicts between individuals or ideas. "We used to think this… but now we think this." "You believe that… but the truth is different… and here's why." These are all hints at dramatic narrative and will help the audience to engage with the content and bridge the gap. If you don't give your presentation a narrative, the audience will make one for you.

– *Focus*. When you stand up you will be given focus. To keep it you must connect with the audience, look at them; really engage with their eyes and you will keep their focus and be able to direct their attention. When you stop they will continue to watch for what you say next – if you are connected by eye contact.

– *Actions*. Acting is action. You are always acting *on* someone – trying to *do* something to them *with* what you are saying. Trying to delight them, fascinate them, shock them, seduce them. The intention need not be related to the content directly. You can delight them with some shocking information; you can intrigue them with something simple. If you are always trying to provoke some clear response from them you will be performing with enough energy to bridge the gap.

Pity the poor punters: the passive audience

The visual, in architecture, statuary and organized triumph, has always been the artistic friend of the dictator. The paucity of business language and the rapid evolution of business argot have deprived many of the ability to express the complexities of their position and to think about, and articulate, creative solutions. We are often participating in live events where the performers are relatively inarticulate and the audience frustrated and dumb. We need to examine what this means, in terms of the types of experience and the styles of thinking that are encouraged by live events. Business life is full of live events – meetings, presentations, conferences – where the closeness to theater is often quite obvious. But the relegation of language, and the dominance of visual imagery, whether that be the PowerPoint presentation or the television interview, coupled with the habit of behaving like a detached spectator, obliged to observe in silence, has radical implications for our ability to notice and articulate nuances of meaning.

The separation of audience and performer brought about by changes in the theater and now taken to the final extreme of television where the audience can shout and boo at the screen alone, unheard and unobserved, has done something very strange to our ability to communicate and to be understood. We depend, I suspect, much more than we did, on gossip and rumor. There has been a surge in the number and popularity of television shows that feature "ordinary people" and allow the public to interact and influence the outcome of the dramas they are watching. Trust in government and turnout at elections have declined dramatically in the last ten years. People are turning more and more to blogs and websites for news and opinions. The powerless audience has finally become deeply suspicious of the managed performance. We tend to trust more and more unreliable and individual sources.

The converse of this is that anyone without training and experience of live performance who gets up on a stage, delivers a presentation, or appears in a television program can become terrified of the audience, oblivious of them, or even resentful. There is little understanding of the fact that communication is co-created, that the audience matter, that what they think and feel from moment to moment matters and needs to be heard and taken into consideration even if the convention means they do not speak.

The famous Brazilian director Augusto Boal tells a story about running a workshop in a prison. He was trying to explain the origins of theater in the time of the ancient Greeks. He explained that initially there had been a protagonist and a chorus and the protagonist would speak to the audience: "This is monologue, one person talking on their own." Then he explained that the antagonist was introduced, so now there was dialog. "What do you suppose dialog is?" he asked. "Two people talking on their own," came the reply. Live communication needs to be a dialog in the true sense, even if the audience happen to be silent.

If you wanted to be entertained in a theater before the nineteenth century, you could not avoid the fact that you were at some level participating in a dialog, a conversation, either with your fellow members of the audience, or with the actors. The idea of the audience sitting in the dark and watching the stage in silence is a new thing. Prior to the nineteenth century the audience were lit and often extremely vocal and active, even leaping on stage to fight with the cast. It was the actor David Garrick in the eighteenth century who pioneered the idea that an audience should shut up and listen. The passive and reverential silence in which today's actors can indulge themselves is a new phenomenon, as, of course, is the cinema, where our surrogates on the screen can unfold their stories oblivious of our responses.

The advantage of this passivity in the audience is that playwrights and performers can get away with much more subtle and delicate explorations of life; it also means they are unlikely to be booed off the stage if their work is rubbish. But the dumb audience has its dangers; among them the opportunity to articulate ideas, and to command attention for them, is confined to a few. The envy and hatred of celebrities that seem to fester just under the surface of the tabloid gossip columns may be an expression of the frustration increasingly felt by those who no longer have a voice, not even as members of an audience. People offer themselves as fodder for exploitative reality TV because they want to have a voice, they want their problems, ideas, life to be examined and regarded too. Their responses to what they were watching before were not heard or seen. And of course they are still not; participation in the performance can leave them feeling manipulated or betrayed. The way they look to others can come as a shock.

There is also a world of difference between the process of performing on the live stage and performing for the camera. When you are acting on film or television, while the principle of acting as action is still the same, there is less of a difficulty in the problem of the physical gap between you and the audience. When you are filming the only other people there are the crew and they are not in the role of an audience. They are not bringing their imagination and active creativity to the party as a theater audience are. They are there to observe technical things. In artistic terms they are responsible for examining the negative space around the performance: observing the backgrounds to ensure they are always reinforcing the visual power of the moment in a way consistent with the director's vision.

So acting for the cameras allows for a much more introspective and reflective technique. Film acting does indeed need to be more about inner emotional states. There is the intermediary of the cameras and the editing suite working on the audience's behalf to select and focus their attention on this flicker of an eyelid, on that almost inaudible intake of breath. Films are made in the editing suite out of the rough sketches, the raw materials that the actors provide. Film actors are not, in the same way a stage actor is, directly responsible for the audience's felt experience of the moment. In terms of analogies, therefore, and possibly in terms of day-to-day usefulness, it is the techniques of stage acting that are more relevant for life and for leadership. For a great deal of a person's impact in the world is down to their ability to influence the felt experience of those around them.

The project of theater from a director's point of view is to try and ensure as nearly as possible that everyone has the same experience of the communication and comes away with the same understanding, and that at any moment all the audience are in the same emotional and intellectual position regarding what they are watching, that they are having a "shared experience." On the rare occasions this happens it is a wonderful thing. It happens most easily when people laugh. We can hear and see that we are all in the same happy place. And, sometimes, the deep silence of an audience in a tragedy can indicate a profound, shared moment of distress; although in this case, of course, they may just be asleep.

CHAPTER 11

The Script

Euro-blather, business-speak and other languages

It may surprise those outside the theater that there is any room for creative emergence in a play. In a conventional play there is a script; everything that is going to be said and is going to happen has been written down. The constraints are very tight. But of course it is not just the content of what you say that has an impact in a communication: it is the intention behind it.

There is everyday communication and there is art. What seems to me to have happened is that these two things have drifted dangerously far apart. As in evolution, two things once connected have become isolated from each other; these increasingly isolated communities have begun to evolve in different directions. Theater and oratory and eloquent speech and poetry have been separated off from business and politics and the marketplace. Politics, business and the marketplace have begun to evolve their own versions of theater and poetry, their own language even. We have a classic case of divergence.

But we are not talking about continental drift here. We are utterly enmeshed and mutually dependent and yet there is gulf emerging between those who are in the thriving global economy (which is rapidly evolving its own language and cultural forms) and the rest, who are still engaged in a local culture with local language and shared understanding. The same is true for science, where there is a growing gulf between the technically literate and the rest who, even if they have access to technology, have no idea how it works. There is an increasingly dangerous rift appearing between the people who inhabit these elite worlds and "speak the language" and the rest of the species who do not share any of it.

The flight from eloquence, while understandable in an egalitarian, homogenized, society also has some dangerous pitfalls. As PowerPoint has aided and abetted the diminution of eloquence, so email and texting has had the same effect on written communication. And it is not just the form of the presentation that has implications for the effects of our communications, but also the specific words we use. A parallel English is emerging, which, while universally understood, is much simpler than the language of the English or Americans. Shakespeare had a vocabulary of

21,000 words, compared with the average English speaker who uses about 2,000. The vocabulary of international business English is even smaller. One of the many striking differences I find between the business world and the arts is the paucity of imagery and the strange argot that permeates business communication. In large international organizations this problem is compounded by the universal use of Euro-Business-English, a dwarf form of British English with a radically reduced vocabulary and a strange grammar.

Below is an email from an industrial client, a charming man of great integrity, describing the circumstances of a group of managers with whom I was about to work. This is a real email, from a specific company but could be applied to practically any group, in any industry. I have copied it below, exactly as I received it; then I have expanded it, reordering it into sentences and paragraphs, and then I have expanded it to read like English-English and not like Euro-Business-English.

Below it is exactly as received:

Couple of things that are important to consider:
–   Operations is under pressure, in terms of service and costs (and this trade-off is not always easy to make).
–   Our strategy is to focus more on a global picture, expand the company in emerging markets, BUT we are willing to spend a lot of money to acquire the companies, but we do not have the culture, plans and people to stabilise, transform and integrate.
–   The focus of the event will be on The Global Experience (Globalco-operation, standards, solutions, methodologies, communities of practice, common systems and so on.) However, ops people are quite busy in there [sic] local environment and do not always have the time or flexibility (read support from management) to look over the fence (This is a difficult ine to address).
–   There is some history in the business unit. New faces, two different units became one, not yet a team atmosphere and an environment that support can be expected from your coll. (Only on a very local level, this does exist). So all in all, a lot to be addressed.
best regards

Below I have pushed it together into sentences and short paragraphs.

As a member of the senior management, I am responsible for putting the people who work in the operations departments, under pressure to deliver a good or improved service to customers, while at the same time making them cut the cost of doing this and reducing the resources I give them to do it with. This makes it very difficult for them.

Meanwhile the people who own and run the company and the senior managers are really only interested in expanding the company over the whole world: particularly in areas like India, China and South America. We are able and willing to spend a lot of money buying new companies in these areas, but we are not making plans, employing any people or spending any of our time working out how we are going to make these new companies work alongside the main business that we already have in Europe.

In the two days we have set aside for this event, we want the operations managers mentioned above to think about, and start to do something about, the problems we have generated as a result of buying new companies around the world. For example: we want them to do something about global cooperation; to work out how to maintain good standards across the whole world, and to find reliable solutions to new business problems. We want them to make sure that all these different new companies use the same methods and that all their information and accounting systems, for example, are using the same technologies and processes, and that everyone knows how they work.

However, as already mentioned, these people are under a lot of pressure simply to fulfil the daily demands we make of them and we do not give them enough resources or support to do what they do now. As a result they do not have the time or the inclination even to look at this set of problems, let alone take responsibility for fixing them.

Also: we have just imposed a major reorganization of these people's work, in order to reduce costs. We have just fired some of them and moved other people into different jobs. We have put groups of people together who at best don't know each other and, at worst, actively mistrust and dislike one another – only in a few, small, departments are there people who are relatively content.

So: all in all, a lot to be addressed.

By making the email into complete sentences, it is possible to create a very powerful story, which may or may not reflect the reality of the situation. Someone else could create another from the same bones. "Business-speak" has no authorial voice and so it is easy to evade responsibility for what is being said. The "short note" form allows for evasion, and the removal of the subjective "I" specifically evades responsibility for what is being said. Writing in "business-speak" manages to evade all the implications of what is really at stake and who may really be responsible. These details matter.

The inability to express complex ideas or nuanced feelings provokes frustration. This shrinking of the language makes it even easier for communication to collapse into bullying or evasion, the hallmarks of the inarticulate. More and more vital communication is taking place between people who are denied the possibility of being vividly, or subtly, expressive because they have a limited vocabulary and are denied the ease and passion that they can call upon when speaking their mother tongue.

Lack of time and a fashion for bold action over considered thought have lead to a language of abbreviation. The spread of PowerPoint throughout the business world and beyond has been a contributory factor in this dangerous shriveling up of our powers of communication. The bullet-point list has replaced the sentence as the unit for constructing an argument and the consequences are profound. PowerPoint is a wonderful tool for telling simple stories. Simple stories have impact. They are great for selling. They are not good for conveying a complex truth.

Here are some more examples from a group of managers in a company, who were invited to describe the objectives of their international team prior to a strategy meeting. Very few had English as a first language:

– "Synchronize our business 100 per cent with CMO – so we create maximum output."

– "Get the local teams to inspire each other with best practices and establish cross country networks – actively – in order to climb the experience curve faster."

– "Moving to experience driven sales mode."

– "Continuing to challenge our global organization to deliver the tools that enable us to compete and hit target."

These are direct quotes. They are not complete nonsense. But they have very little power to move or inspire and they are general to the point of uselessness. They could be applied to any business anywhere in the world. They are written in haste, in business English, with its short forms and hanging participles, and they convey only the most clichéd and hackneyed ideas. If these really are the kinds of ideas that they are all flying around the world to meet and discuss, then God help their organization.

They might as well be saying:

– "We need to be getting better and not getting worse."

– "We need to sell more stuff if we want to sell more stuff."

In art it is always the concrete and the specific, the telling detail, wherein resides the power of any work of art. This note – this chord, at this point – not that one, this spot of paint – exactly here – this word here, not that one. Without it, art has no power. Writing has no power.

The danger of business language is that it cannot contain the variety that is in the room. Everyone can attend the meeting, happily sign up to the agreed list of actions and leave with radically different perceptions of what has been discussed and what the actions agreed really imply. Dealing with the consequences of this divergence, and the handling of status games and ego conflicts, probably consumes most of the energy of anyone in a large organization. And these are organizations with a thrilling level of diversity. If only people could communicate properly the creative potential would be enormous.

The telling detail: rediscovering the power of words

In acting, and probably in all art, there is an obsession with concrete detail. There is a similar obsession in business, but it seems that people use the science model and therefore feel they need to measure something before they can work with it, as if the important facts of a situation are only those properties that can be recorded numerically. In theater work the text is crucial. The relationship with "the facts," or more accurately "the givens," is a subtle and central one. Working alone, choosing the telling detail is hard enough. In ensemble work it is harder still because in ensemble work you have to work with the complex truth that exactly the same "facts" will mean different things to everyone in the room. This diversity is both the raw material of your creative process and a profound challenge to the director's ability to author the piece.

The detail matters, even when you are looking at the big picture. In fact it matters more when you are looking at a big picture. Not all the detail, though: sometimes a thing can be rough and general and it won't matter, sometimes it can be cut out altogether, but sometimes it must be exact – the telling detail. The brushwork on a painting of a gown may be loose and generalized; there is room for variation there. But the tiny point of light that is reflected off the edge of the clasp that gathers the gown at the wearer's neck is exactly right – one millimeter to the left or right and the illusion would not come together. Put exactly *there*, and that precise size and shape, and that tiny dot of paint makes the whole generalized mass look exactly like a gown.

In art there is no hierarchy of details. Even though the actor who says "The queen, my lord, is dead" has a small role to play; without that line at that point, the play would fall apart. In facilitating sessions around strategy, or planning, or "blue-sky thinking," there is often a sense of irritation with detail. We want to get the broad direction right, we want to iron out the general concepts and then worry about the detail, but in art that doesn't work. You always proceed with the detail in mind. Often a vision in your head, about a production or a poem or a picture, will be only a detail, a specific but resonant fragment of a possible future that you know has an undiscovered context, which it is your task to reveal.

As you proceed, it is often the awkward detail that emerges as you work that provides a creative constraint that unlocks the whole project. This inverse phenomenon is just as important as the telling detail that the artist wants to make happen. Work on a project can often be mostly a quest for the detail that will unlock the problem. This can be a knot in the wood you are carving, an unexpected attack of the giggles in a serious scene you are rehearsing, or it can be the unexpected choice of a word or a phrase in a poem or a piece of text. The telling detail is the point at which the possible becomes concrete.

Here are some statements from a strategy meeting I attended for a company, in which I had been invited to make only a small contribution. The "team" were engaged in a bit of "blue-sky thinking" about their future and had been specifically asked to think about the question "What will this organization look in ten years' time?" There were operations managers in the room from the whole European division of the organization, all Hamlets. As I walked around the room, ideas were pouring out of them onto flipcharts – first thoughts, abundant and half-baked, in a great, creative torrent. There was enthusiasm and excitement in the room. Here are a couple of examples I carefully selected from the many I saw:

– "Will have a Chinese CEO! "

– "Enough TRAINED freighter pilots!"

In this particular case there must have been about five hundred statements of this kind created by the large (mostly white, mostly male, middle-aged) group. Having produced this torrent of material they were then guided through a meticulous and rigorous process of great integrity, designed to reduce this unmanageable torrent to a few general manageable principles. After much work, and a palpable waning of enthusiasm and excitement, some fundamental statements were produced:

– "Will have a Chinese CEO!" became "We will be a diverse organization. "

– "Enough TRAINED freighter pilots!" became "We will have an international reach."

The diversity and creative abundance of the first phase of the work had been swiftly drained of its power and reduced to a handful of lifeless platitudes. Of course there must be a process of selection after the first creative splurge, but not this one, this dull logic of working methodically, as a scientist might, from the particular to the general in a classic reductive process. There were probably five other statements, out of the original flood of ideas, that could, if realized, have produced all the organization's strategic objectives as a byproduct of pursuing a handful of carefully chosen details. In order to deliver all of the imagined performance, all that is required is to fully embody the right detail.

Setting about the process of ensuring that in ten years' time your organization did, definitely, have a Chinese CEO, would lead to the kind of active (and controversial) changes that "being a diverse organization" would never inspire. As an objective it allows you all the freedom you could want, to invent and to build and to adapt to what emerges, but it keeps you clearly focused in the right direction, in a way that is exciting and inspiring. The telling detail can crystallize the whole enterprise.

But it has to be the right one. Someone has to choose, and someone has to watch the progress of the attempt to enact it and direct that progress from moment to moment. The concrete, specific objective is, like a good poem, imaginable: you can visualize it clearly, it will not leave you, and it resonates immediately with all sorts of images and implications. It is a good creative constraint: it sets you to work at once with a clear objective.

When Kasper Bech Holten was appointed artistic director of the Royal Danish Opera, the youngest person ever to fill that position, he created a mission statement for the opera house. It was this: "At the Royal Danish Opera we make people cry." This specific concrete objective was all that was required. It told the artists and the potential audience the tenor of the work – there would be no cold, intellectual, experiences here. It told the staff what kind of experience they were helping to create at all levels. It even allowed the ushers to think about bringing in spare handkerchiefs for the audience, just in case. It was not elitist, neither was it a vague, general aspiration; it was concrete and, of course, measurable.

In acting and probably in all art, there is an obsession with finding the telling detail. There is a similar obsession with detail in business but people approach detail as scientists do. They feel that they need to understand some general principle before they can do work on detail; or that the detail is a by-product of the operation of general principles; that it comes about as a result of, or gets in the way of, the operation of stable and repeatable processes. Detail in art is not at the bottom of a hierarchy of principles; it is right in the middle of the creative process and enfolds the principles within it. The telling detail is a reflecting shard of the whole work.

Truth, lies and presentations

Many situations in life are difficult to understand. The inability to talk about them in a way that truthfully reflects their complexity is already having catastrophic consequences for our business and political life. Public discourse is awash with cliché, with soundbites, with hackneyed metaphors, with clunky business-speak. But this simplification of rhetoric is very useful for power and control. It is one way of limiting the creative emergence that happens within all communication. "To do nothing is not an option" is a typical thumping cliché. It is simple, unambiguous, inelegant – and false.

Colin Powell famously presented to the UN a story about nuclear weapons in Iraq that was highly plausible – and completely untrue. Colin Powell's presentation was highly theatrical, it had snatches of recorded dialog and was full of concrete details about the characters in the little exchanges that were played out before the audience. It landed powerfully and convincingly on the audience. It swept away the subtle, nuanced and ambiguous truth that was being told by Hans Blix, the UN weapons inspector.

But Hans Blix had engaged in a dialog. He did not give a presentation; he read a report and then answered questions. If people want the truth from someone, they tend to believe that a dialog, a cross-examination, is more likely to yield it. It is the power of the debate. It allows for the forensic reduction of complexity and potential to a single certainty, which one fervently hopes is the truth.

Courtrooms, parliamentary committees, senate hearings, examining magistrates, interrogators – all understand, that people under examination must not be allowed to perform a rehearsed speech if they are to avoid the danger of being manipulated or deceived. Allow people to rehearse and present to you, and they will be able to do what the theater does. They will be able to craft a performance that will bring the whole audience to that same point of understanding. They will be able to sell you a story. And stories can be fiction or fact.

This is a very powerful tool. In the service of art, it allows for the revelation of complexity, and perhaps resonant insight. It can do this in politics or business too but it depends, radically, on the virtue of the performer and the integrity of the project. The spread of "presentation" as the default mode of communication in business may have interesting consequences. It can just as easily be used to deprave, deceive and corrupt as it can be used to enlighten, inspire and inform. If we know how it works, we might be able to use it safely.

"Communication skills" are the most powerful weapon in the hands of a leader but they are a double-edged sword. They are, in themselves, only a set of craft skills that can be taught to anyone and used by anyone to create the illusion of truth, or the illusion of leadership.

CHAPTER 12

Rehearsing for Business and for Life

One way of describing theater is to call it a shared experience. A bunch of people go into a theater and settle down to enjoy the show. The story unfolds, they get involved and at some point something happens and they all laugh at the same time. It's a good feeling. In a tragedy sometimes you hear the muffled sobs, too often the muffled snores. These shared experiences can be cathartic and crucial for us, whether we get them in the theater or the football ground or the political rally. They are an acknowledgement that we agree, we understand one another – we are among those who think and feel like us. There is an element of this sort of theater in business meetings.

When you are trying to create these experiences in the theater you can't test what you are doing and sometimes you can get it wrong. You find you have made an experience that can be shared only among yourselves. Other people looking at the same scene acted out in the same way feel something quite different. This is always a risk when you are making art. But it is a risk everywhere. It is very easy for people to read the same events in quite different ways; it is easy for leaders and managers to proceed in the belief that their views are shared when they are not. Audiences in the theater and audiences for business meetings can sometimes be fatally polite.

The Brazilian theater director Augusto Boal has a method that opens a window into how the creative process in a group works, and provides a practical process for conducting the kinds of dialog you need, if you want to discover and to develop ideas rather than have them compete with one another. In a nutshell, Boal's core idea was to break down the barrier between audience and actor and have the spectators – or "spectactors," as Boal called them – intervene in the scenario being performed – to make them active participants in the drama, to interact and role-play in a situation and so assert their views of the issues being enacted before them. These early ideas are explored in detail in his work on the "Theater of the Oppressed" (Boal 1992) – a phrase that explains much of Boal's political and philosophical approach to his work.

I want to look in detail at just one technique from what Boal calls his "arsenal of the Theater of the Oppressed." Not because it is the only or the recommended approach – far from it – but because I have used it with some success in business and because I think it points a way to developing an approach to the whole idea of meetings that could provide businesses and organizations with a tool that will allow them to rehearse, like soldiers and actors do. Not to "plan and implement," or to "discuss" or "strategize," but to "rehearse" – to explore, in a concrete and practical way, the options before them, to make and try out possible futures, and test their behavior, in order to find the best one.

Image theater as a tool for organizations

One of the techniques Boal uses to achieve this transfer of initiative to the spectators is called "image theater" and involves people in a group creating frozen images or tableaux using the people and objects in the room. You could perhaps look at it as a visual debate. He gives many examples in his books (Boal 1992, 1995), but the process has some interesting constraints that make it a process very different from the default mode of competitive advocacy that people tend to fall back on in discussions.

When making images for image theater, the person who is modeling the tableaux of scenes or situations is not allowed to speak; they are constrained to use the others in the group like modeling clay and silently form them into an image. There are many ways of doing this and the process can be collaborative or individual, but the ones that deny speech often produce the most interesting results.

I have used this technique as a consultancy tool to great effect. When working with a group of managers I will sometimes ask them to make an image of what is holding them back at work, or an abstract image of how the things that are blocking them feel, or an image of something quite concrete like a process within the organization or the organization as a whole.

A group of managers on an awayday have been invited to construct an image in response to the question "What is holding me back from achieving my objectives?"

One woman creates an image using three of her colleagues in her group: she makes an image of herself seated with her hands out in front of her, as if they are typing on a keyboard. She positions her colleagues so that they are standing behind her pressing down on her head with their hands.

The interesting bit comes with the interpretation of the images. You can encourage people to make a series of images in small groups and then to show the images like sculptures in a gallery. The rest of the group then gathers round to look and comment. Boal then disciplines this discussion in an interesting way: he draws a clear and sharp distinction between the objective and the subjective comments. It is essential that we learn to separate the description of what we see from the interpretation we make of what we see.

First people are invited to make objective comments about the images that can be incontestable, for example:

- "There are three people in the group; one is seated, the others are standing behind the seated figure pressing down on their head with both hands."

- "The person on the chair has their hands in front of them with their fingers splayed."

- "No one is looking at anyone else."

These are the facts. The image is then interpreted and wild free association encouraged:

- "It looks like I feel when I am trying to write a report with a hangover!"

- "They are pushing her down in her seat – she wants to get away!"

- "She's trying to play the piano and they don't want her to stop."

- "Her brain is trying to float away and they are keeping it in!"

- "It's the line managers getting her down."

- "She's had a bad hair day and they are two emergency hairdressers come to save her!"

When people venture these crazy suggestions they sometimes sound as if they have seen the right answer. They sometimes are quite convinced that they have the "correct" interpretation. At this stage they are encouraged to preface everything they say with "It looks to me as if … " This simple discipline gradually transforms the relations within the group as they practice on and work with other images and occasionally hear from those who want to say what the image they have made means to them. They withdraw to more tentative positions, they venture their interpretations with an increased understanding that in this area there are no right answers.

Buried in each of these interpretations is some kind of resonance. Each one is refiguring the same information in different ways. Each spectator is weaving what they see in front of them into their own story and coloring it with their own ideas and obsessions. This always happens: we cannot stop ourselves from doing it, but this process makes it obvious and brings out the alternative, quirky and individual slants on the situation that we all have. This variety is the soil in which originality and innovation can be grown. To the person who has made the image, this flood of alternative visions can be strangely enlightening, and sometimes the interpretations can lead to ideas about how the person who made the image may solve their problem.

There is no need for the person who made the image to reveal the "real" or "true" interpretation of the image if they don't want to, so it can be a useful and safe tool for exploring personal dilemmas at work.

(In this case of the image of the woman on the chair, her brain trying to fly away struck a cord with the person who had made the image, who was able to reflect on the fact that it was not so much the people she felt were pressurizing her at work that were the problem; she could handle that. Her resentment was more about the fact that her mind never had time to float free. What she specifically resented was the lack of thinking time rather than the pace of work as such. This allowed her to reorganize her schedule outside of work for dreaming time and to accept the pressure (which she knew was short-term) more equably.)

The trap of ambiguity

Image theater makes it possible to work with a reality that is often suppressed in business life: the reality that we all have a different inner world and a different internal explanation for and attitude to events. We can be aligned to an extent but the difference of internal perception will remain. Yet these differences are both the source of creativity and the cause of much distress in groups that work together. "Real" total alignment cannot be achieved; only a stance of receptivity to others and commitment to tackling the task is possible.

The same image resonates differently for each of us and we respond in a many-layered way. In theater this divergence is minimized by the separation of the audience from the actors – by the ritual space. But the seeds of this process are inherent in every interaction. We are responding to a continuous stream of clues and signals and constructing stories about each other from them all the time – and being wrong, and being misled, and re-establishing understanding, and coming closer or driving one another apart. In theater this contested territory is where we work – in the ritual space defined between the actors (the protagonists), the audience and the director, or leader.

Business life is full of ritualized moments – meetings, presentations, briefings and so on – and each one of us is both participating in and interpreting theses scenes as they unfold before us. It is dangerously easy, if we are the leader – sitting in the director's or manager's chair – to believe that our interpretation of what is unfolding is the "right" one. We are always in danger of believing that everyone sees what we see or of believing that what we see is correct, definitive. It is equally easy to fall into the role of passive audience and create a meaning in our heads that we do not communicate back to the actors. One of the great values of the image theater process is that it allows us to *show* what a situation looks like to us rather than to tell it. It makes clear the theatrical nature of these events and the different roles we are obliged to take from moment to moment.

When we speak in a group it is very easy for us to co-create. We have to proceed on the assumption that people, more or less, see what we see or we would find it hard to communicate at all, but even in the simplest matters there is always more divergence than we like to admit, and in order to stay in the group and avoid rejection we often pretend we agree and see the same thing, even when we are not so sure we really do. This is "group-think," both necessary for community and fatal for communication.

We are less likely in a "discussion" to speak in a quirky or individual way. We will tend to normalize our speech, fall in with the agreed argot and use it to make what we say acceptable. We become masters of contemporary rhetoric and try to "sell" our ideas rather than offer them for completion by other views. The complex play of status, allegiance and enmity in the group shapes what we find we can say. And of course the least articulate and lowest-status individuals often find themselves unheard.

When we are constrained by the image technique to make an image of what we think, two things happen. We begin to think in parallel, rather than attempting to line up our thoughts, and we also find ourselves forced to be ambiguous and/or metaphorical, so as a result we often include material that we would not normally include if we were to try to speak our minds rather than show them.

There is a huge pressure against ambiguity in the work situation, for all sorts of good and obvious reasons. But when we are looking at complex issues, and – vitally if we want to find new solutions to old problems – if we want any degree of creativity in the workplace then we need ambiguity. It has often been said that the hallmark of the creative mind is to be able to tolerate ambiguity – to suspend our disbelief, to withhold judgment. It is hard enough to practice these skills at the best of times, but under the pressure of deadlines and appraisals it is often impossibly hard. It also seems to conflict with our established images of leaders as decisive and able to act quickly and with certainty.

The irony is that much time is spent in organizations and in life generally in dealing with the consequences of being decisive and then discovering that your decision impinged on something you didn't see or understand at the time, or that the consequences were radically different in its implications for the other people you are working with. If you invite people to show metaphorically, in a theatrical or artistic way, what they mean, if you use images alongside words (and the more abstract and metaphorical the methods the better), you actually have a process that is much better and faster than trying to work in a linear fashion, precisely because it includes ambiguity and metaphor. Arts-based methods, like Boal's image theater, can include the felt context of the decisions. The difficult and unsayable can be shown and its implications can be considered by the group in silence, in their own contexts.

If the group is then invited to work collaboratively on building a solution in a metaphorical form, in a model or a picture rather than in a list of actions, the images can contain all the ambiguous complexity that exists in reality. The models and images can become shared shorthand for a complex solution to a complex problem. This use of intelligent metaphor is not "shorthand" for the detailed preparation of lists and matrices; it is the robust and right methodology for exploring and communicating complex ideas. It is a method for the rapid prototyping of strategy.

I am advocating this particular methodology because it is one I have used and because I think it needs to be developed. I have had few opportunities to use it and it requires a considerable leap of faith and imagination to dare to apply it and, more important, to trust the strange output as being as reliable as the outcome of more conventional processes, or even more so. I am also advocating it because I have only just begun to see that some of the insights provided by these sessions actually were far more revealing than I and the participants realized at the time (see Shaw 2002).

I worked with the senior management of a global oil company some years ago when they were riding high. We made a series of images of the whole enterprise and I remember vividly the moment when there was a conversation sparked by some of the group who were representing the upstream part of the business and someone from the downstream part who was trying to manipulate their part of the image to reflect their priorities. I, and I think many others in the group, could see that there was a faultline here in the agreed image of the company. There was something amiss, some tension and ambiguity between the visions of these two elements. The image was quite detailed and now, some years later, I can recall it clearly. The image exposed a faultline in the company that indeed yielded an expensive and nearly catastrophic failure a few years later.

Image theater may be a very powerful and effective consultancy tool if given the chance to grow. As one client reported, after a prolonged intervention using this technique:

- "It deals with the intangibles, not what you can write down on paper."
- "You feel able to express your views in a non-confrontational way."
- "You can explore off-the-wall ideas, without being branded a radical."
- "It's like holding a picture in your head rather than words."
- "It's not a problem solver, it's a solution finder."

It also has some advantages that other theater-based interventions don't have. "Forum theater" is now used quite widely in business. In forum theater a group of actors will perform a play based on the organization's life and the audience will be invited to participate in the performance and discuss and role-play different scenarios or solutions to the problems presented in the performance. This is a very powerful and effective tool for raising and discussing issues.

There is, however, a potential danger in that the original play must be written, rehearsed and performed by someone, and it is easy in this process for the content to be presented in a way that does not access the true "unsayables" – what has sometimes been referred to as "Boal lite" – the production of interventions that, either consciously or unconsciously, presented the prevailing management view and were a tool for training and development, rather than a really creative forum for expressing the dangerous or the unknown. The risk – and the exciting potential – of image theater is that all the material is generated in the room by the people involved, that it is much harder to control the agenda and much easier for the genuinely surprising or dangerous to emerge. Without that possibility, that element of real risk, there is unlikely to be any real innovation or new insight.

Case study: the shooting party

I had the opportunity to work with a group from an organization that were attempting a major reorganization of one of their departments. A day out was planned. One of the first things we did was to take the "organizational tree" of the department and reprint it upside down. This helped us to ensure that we got the right cast of characters in the room and had enough representation from all levels of the organization. We put together a cast of characters that represented all the different threads of the organizational story. (As with a Shakespeare play, you do not need to have the whole British army on stage, but you do need to see a couple of soldiers having a fight or a conversation about their lives in order fully to understand the drama that is being played out.)

We then went away together and worked for half a day to build an ensemble. The work went well and by the second day hierarchical differences were duly suspended. "Support staff" were duly bonded with senior managers (including two members of the board). We then embarked on an intensive rehearsal process using image theater and a lot of lively conversation, to make tableaux and images of how the department looked now and how it could look in the future.

The first image was volunteered by the head of department. He placed all the members of the department in rows, like footballers having their team photograph taken. After some hesitation he then placed himself on a chair standing behind and above the group with his arms outstretched in a gesture of enclosure.

The next image was made by one of the (almost entirely female) support staff in the group. Here is what she made:

Six men are standing in a loose group; all are facing in the same direction and looking off into the distance. Kneeling on the floor beside each of them is a woman, looking up at the man.

One of the men standing included the head of the department. The image was greeted in silence by the group. Someone said: "They look like a group of men out on a shooting party with their gundogs at their heels." There was a palpable sense in the room that an important "unsayable" about the culture of the department and the values it expressed had been "voiced." The image was shockingly different from that made by the head of department.

There was no need to say more, to meet and discuss and make representations; the power of the image was overwhelming and said all that needed to be said. This led to an admission that one of the problems in the department was a frankly sexist tendency to undervalue the contribution of the (mostly female) support staff and a failure to utilize their potential. After this breakthrough we quickly arrived at a new shape for the organization of the department. This included redefining people's roles, relocating individuals and departments to different parts of the country, and changing the way in which people reported in and shared information.

We tried out images of how the structure could work and, in that experimental, playful process, discovered and confronted the realities of relocating individuals, changing the balance of power and responsibility. We improvised the way in which these new conversations might sound. People tried out the idea of talking more freely and closely to some people, and reflected on the implications of having less contact with someone else. They rehearsed their future. They did not plan it, or talk about it, or list it as action points to be done later and somewhere else. They tried it out, in a rough way, in the room with all the relevant people represented. They were able to speak on behalf of all those affected by the proposals and also able to directly modify the proposals as they emerged from the ensemble.

It then took six months for the organization to do anything. Eventually the scenario that we had co-created at the first rehearsals was enacted. Afterwards, I asked the leader and champion of the project why they had not just gone ahead and implemented what we had made that first day. He said "We could have done, but we didn't believe it was possible to reach a solution that fast."

CHAPTER 13

Training for Creative Leadership

Apprenticeship, mastery and transcendence

Most of the skills of effective leadership and good management are embodied knowledge, not intellectual: charm, decisiveness, compassion, enthusiasm, persuasiveness, the ability to listen, to be firm, to establish boundaries for others, to inspire. Such activities are mostly to do with being expressive, with being able to induce, in others, feelings and emotions aligned with the actions required of them. Encouraging patience and thoughtfulness in others is also an action that needs to be partly embodied. In the arts, it is only after mastery of the embodied skills has been achieved that a practitioner transcends their training and innovates.

What would be the embodied skills that a group of people might need to master in this way to work as leaders in other fields? What are, and where would one learn, the embodied skills of teamworking, or leadership, or innovation: the craft of business? I can learn about music or go to a creative writing course, but I could not, on the basis of that, call myself a craftsman or an artist. I would have only the most superficial ability in the field. What would the skills of the leader or manager be that could be developed in this way?

For when I work in organizations it is in the physical skills of leadership that I see the greatest lacks: of decisiveness, of persuasiveness, of the ability to listen and reflect, to set constraints, to play – or desist from – status games, to support, encourage, enrage or inspire as need be. Organizations seem to me to spend most of their time and energy dealing with inappropriate, unexpressed and poorly directed feelings and behaviors. That target-setting has been a disaster in some organizations has been partly because the targets and goals are "cold" – they are just numbers, and so become hated abstractions rather than embodied motivations. They also allow managers to control the work their people do, without having to engage with them emotionally. This is a great relief for them, but it misses an opportunity: the opportunity to arouse the passions that accompany masterful achievement.

Sometimes when we see a successful leader at work we get a sense of masterful craftsmanship. It has something to do with what we describe as "natural authority" or "charisma" or "charm" or "presence." It seems to me that success as a leader or manager is almost entirely about our ability to handle personal relationships, to read and judge and "handle" people – as if people were the clay, the paint, the medium, of our craft. Where do we learn to practice "handling people" with the sensitivity and perception of an artist – and who should be our teachers?

Evidently there are people who have a talent for it and, as in all art forms, the talented almost always rise to the top. The untalented may also rise but in general, outstanding talent in any field is self-evident and with only minimal encouragement, can be identified and fostered. The tragedy of our education system is that even this minimal attention is sometimes not there and is often not there for those whose exceptional talents may not lie at the heart of our creaky old academic values: talents for empathy, talents for visualization, talents for imaginative projection, talents for music, dance, politics, drawing, fieldwork, acting, and so on. What is intriguing is that in this area of "handling people," which seems to be the pre-eminent requirement of a good manager, there is minimal formal provision.

"Being creative" is seen as something spontaneous and easy and childlike. It is, of course – but there can be no great art without mastery. There is a large difference between the amateur who does it sometimes for love, and the professional who has to do it continuously for money. And the difference may not be a difference of originality or insight but a difference of mastery. The professional, by dint of sheer extra hours of practice, can do things with the medium that the amateur can't, and so they are able to express things more strikingly, more subtly, more beautifully and more truthfully than the amateur. Just because someone has made an effort and produced something original does not mean that it is as good as the work of another, who has made a similar effort but is a master of the medium.

Mastery is achieved by discipline; increasingly this is obliged to be self-discipline. In whatever way we negotiate this difficult territory, there is no escaping the long hours spent at the piano, the aching shoulders wielding the brush, the broken, chafed hands of the sculptor; the days and years of your only life, that every artist – without exception – gives up to their craft, to achieve the mastery that allows them to be expressive in it. This work may be done gladly or reluctantly, it may be done under threat of punishment or in a frenzy of visionary excitement, but it must be done. And it is almost impossible to do it to a level of excellence without a master.

When I work with groups of senior managers I notice that the more senior they are the less likely I am to be able to begin my session on time. I also have to spend much more time and energy getting them to be silent for the exercises to work. This is natural. As people get older and more experienced they may listen less and obey less readily. But when I am working with actors, whatever they may think inside, they will happily engage with the work, however senior they are. They will turn up on time and be silent when asked, straight away. This is just practice, convention if you like, but it is part of the discipline drummed into actors from their early training.

These disciplines are disappearing from the workplace. In throwing out deference and conformity we have also thrown out the conventions of attention and punctuality – details, among many others, that matter if we are to organize and invent swiftly and successfully.

But of course all this discipline and the practice of it become a set of creative constraints in themselves, and how the master frames them and how individuals respond to them makes a difference to the outcomes in terms of the pupil's later achievements. Some become masterful imitators of the taught style, but do not innovate. Some rebel and never become masters. A few are able to absorb and master the taught elements but remain dynamically creative. They are able to respond creatively to the constraints of their craft as given them by their masters and then transcend them.

Apprenticeship, mastery, craftsmanship; these are unfashionable words in today's world of work. They belong to a past in which women had low status and work was divided between the sexes. They describe a medieval progress from apprentice to master. They deny an egalitarian, knowledge-based, economy and refer to a closed, fixed world of hereditary skills and personal relationships. They also describe an education, a growth of the craftsperson from imitator to expert to artist. The master craftsman that transcends what has been achieved before. The only place this language is now safely used is in fantasy fiction. But "mastery" and "apprenticeship" describe a set of relationships and behaviors that are still relevant today.

Underneath the sacrifice necessary to become a master who can transcend the known to innovate, you need to have a deep love of what you are doing. Classical musicians who, eventually, are able to make great music speak directly to our hearts, have to get their fingers to a state of strength and suppleness that can be achieved only by hours and hours and hours and hours of practice. All painters must put paint on canvas for days and weeks and months and years, until their shoulders ache and their eyes smart, writers must churn out millions and millions of words. This can only be done if you are in love with something in your art.

There may be something about the passion and the emotional drama that a master–apprentice relationship can have that is necessary to the transmission of embodied rather than intellectual knowledge. Art means craftsmanship: skill, first and foremost, whether that is in movement or in the manipulation of tools or instruments. And for mastery to be achieved there needs to be practice and discipline. It may be that a level of intensity is essential for the communication of embodied knowledge. It may be necessary to arouse passion, in order to learn how to express it.

However, the master–apprentice model is also about excellence. The medieval guilds both fostered excellence and stifled innovation. They provided a brutal set of constraints and a highly restrictive set of codes that limited how and what could be done. But there is little doubt that they also fostered excellence and supreme mastery. When we look at the work of medieval guild members today they still utterly astound.

It is certainly the case that some of the experiences necessary for acquiring embodied knowledge cannot be had without discipline. For some experiences, silence is essential; for others, intense physical effort. These states will need to be maintained and people need to be pushed there. They will not happily stumble upon the ability to draw a perfect circle or play an arpeggio or dance on point. Acquiring highly sophisticated embodied knowledge requires the presence of a master and the acceptance of the status and power relations implicit in being an apprentice. This may not be true of other forms of knowledge. You can indeed learn a lot from books and from conversation with equals. Autodidacts exist but are rare, and truly outstanding physical performances in the arts are always the result of someone pushing at some stage.

In the craft-based world of art, this progress is the only one you can make. There are no generalists among artists. Someone who is a writer is not then able to transfer that knowledge directly to making beautiful pots or paintings. This is partly because the knowledge that needs to be transferred in training an artist is embodied knowledge. It is kinaesthetic or emotional knowledge as well as intellectual; it is mediated by an understanding of the physical self. You need to get the skills into your body, your fingers – your imagination. And this can only be done experientially.

Many artforms still need this personal master–apprentice form to be taught successfully. Actors and musicians happily attend master-classes with noted practitioners where they still, sometimes literally, sit at the feet of a master and allow themselves to be inspired and sometimes even roundly abused, in order to achieve a higher level of mastery. But there is a tendency to believe now that this strongly hierarchical style of pedagogy is medieval, potentially abusive and redundant. I am not entirely sure.

Of course it is possible to teach with only gentleness and reason, and that is what we should all aspire to. Nevertheless, it is interesting that true mastery, utterly outstanding achievement in a physical skill, is seldom achieved without passionate expression within the master–apprentice relationship. Somewhere people need to be inspired by the towering demands made of them by a master. Within the intense relationship that can exist between a master or mistress and a pupil, this is seldom achieved without, at some stage, high emotion.

Our experience of education, if it is a good one, is almost always associated with a close, personal relationship; some master or mistress, who enthused us with a desire to master some particular subject of study and was then able to transfer to us the skills for doing so. Unfortunately perhaps, these kinds of mistress–pupil or master–apprentice relationships have become suspect. They are blatantly open to abuse and have been roundly abused over the centuries. There is a power structure to them which, as contemporary democrats, we find difficult to deal with. There are deeply worrying parental and sexual overtones to them and they are now a psychological and legislative minefield.

The uncomfortable truth is that these relationships, when they are working well, are full of deep emotion. Teachers fall in love with their pupils, apprentices worship their masters. The danger of tipping over into inappropriate behavior is always there. And when they are not working well, the converse is true. There is a danger of manipulation, cruelty and abuse. People are often reluctant to take on the mantle of the master and people are often uncomfortable and resentful of taking on the lowly role of apprentice or pupil. Unfortunately there is not another way of making the transfer of the embodied knowledge that you need for mastery to be achieved. When we make our education system safe from these dangers we make it less good at fostering excellence and passion, the distinguishing features of the professional artist.

This has worrying implications for both education and business, especially businesses where "creativity and innovation" or "experiences and services" are what is being traded. In Britain we have bet the future on being able to sustain the nation on trading intangibles. We have no natural resources left to speak of (a little coal and oil for a short time); we have no large-scale manufacturing. It matters very much that we are able to educate and manage a society of artists and yet as a nation we are pitifully ignorant of how art is actually made and how artists are actually trained and led. Much of current practice in education and in business encourages and supports the diametric opposite of what is required to develop the artistic mindset, achieve excellence and create tradable works.

There is another fundamental difference between the world of the artist and that of the rest which I will not go into in depth but is equally important to understand. The arts run a gift economy. Within the arts and between artists, plagiarism is understood. In fact it is tacitly encouraged. People allow themselves to be imitated, their ideas taken and adapted. Indeed, ideas are actively given out into the artistic community and handed down between the generations. And no one sues. The other fact is that almost without exception, artists are independent freelance contractors. These fundamentals have radical implications if we are seriously to think about running a "creative economy."

Chapter 14

Art in the World

Audacity and risk-taking

Most of the success of great creative directors lies not only in the power and originality of their ideas but in their ability to manage the creativity of others, to use the constraints of each stage of a project to define the field within which the people will then work. And they are able to present that field as a series of concrete and exciting challenges that will release people into a creative response regardless of the consequences. They are above all vigilant, watching all the time for the fragments of a good idea which they can encourage and support and then weave into their vision for the whole piece.

Most of their skill lies in the way they handle language and the way they handle their authority with others. They are flexible and at ease with any status they are required to play, godlike at one stage, open and unsure at another. But mostly they lead with the humility that comes with a habit of watchfulness and a respect for the fact that an idea can come from anyone, at any time, and may be better than the one you are holding. There is, however, another more important conclusion from this. Directing creativity can be done only by people on the ground, close to the action, which implies that creativity and innovation can be successfully fostered only if the director is working with a relatively small team. The field under observation must be within the locus of influence of the director. You cannot direct creativity from afar.

A number of years ago, BP launched its new corporate slogan, "Beyond Petroleum." On the face of it this is an excellent, creative constraint. It is specific and immediately gets the imagination going. What if an oil company went beyond petroleum and perhaps directed its wealth and resources and skilled personnel towards generating and selling energy that was not petroleum-derived? What will the transport system look like when we have gone beyond petroleum and what will an energy company look like then? It is an exciting constraint. But as it turned out, it didn't work out that way. Very shortly after the slogan was launched in 1999 it became clear that this was not what was actually happening.

The oil price at the time was very low, margins were to be made on the downstream, retail end of the business, and the company had recently acquired some huge refineries as a result of mergers with or acquisition of other companies. "Beyond Petroleum" in the retail end of the business meant coffee shops in petrol stations and a "greener" image. This shift of focus had many unforeseen consequences for the successful integration and management of the newly acquired refining businesses. To go beyond petroleum and become a clean, green energy corporation is a great set of constraints. They are truly stimulating, but they were not effective for several reasons. One was that they were not accepted and explored with the audacity and ambition that they implied, and they were not explored at the level of the ensemble. There is never a blank canvas, and the starting conditions, the cast in the room, will make for a very different emergent journey, depending on where you start. Creative constraints need to be employed at the locus of influence of the director. This may have been true with BP: the constraints may have worked well for the core downstream managers who had most contact with the retail and marketing end of the business; but they did not work so well for the global supply and refining elements. Whatever the case, the potential of the idea enfolded within the proposition "Beyond Petroleum, What if … ?" has not so far been realized.

In the end the slogan worked most successfully as a rebranding, PR intervention. Although it might, with sufficient audacity, have transformed the organization, there seems never to have been the ambition among the leaders of the organization to throw themselves into the imaginative implications of this bold idea and to make them happen.

Being bold

I suspect that the people in British Petroleum never let themselves be fired by the creative constraint that their advertising agency had helped them to describe. They did not allow themselves to be possessed by the consequences of their choice of words, that huge, non-judgmental, fearful, excited anticipation that gets you in the gut just before you go to work. The public, perhaps, felt this excitement on their behalf (I did), which is why it was so successful at the time from the PR point of view. And it highlights the curious separation that exists between businesses and "the creatives" that they hire in from time to time.

One of the consequences of the hierarchy in businesses is that authorial power is not distributed. There is no invitation or preparedness to disseminate authorship (and creativity) through the organization. As a result of this, audacity in business is usually expressed in terms of the big deal, not the courage to charge your people with a daring possibility and watch what they come up with, forging your business out of that. Mega deals, big mergers and acquisitions – the dangerous games of corporate poker that fill the pages of the business press – dominate the corporate world. The same is true of the public sector, where the political motivation for many big change programs is more obvious.

These are the political maneuverings of despots, not the audacious gestures of creative artists, and it has long been established that they are overwhelmingly to do with amassing wealth and power in the hands of a small number of individuals and very little to do with the beauty, utility or functionality of the outcomes. Indeed KPMG produced a report in 1999 demonstrating very clearly that 83 per cent of mergers in the survey made no difference to shareholder value, or actually destroyed it. And the cost of failed or abandoned initiatives by the current UK government is measured in billions of taxpayers' pounds.

How then do you unleash audacious creativity within an organization, and still maintain control of the general direction? What do you dare to do? Artists and artisans work alone or in small groups. It is very hard to take risks on behalf of a large organization and all its dependents and with all its myriad given constraints – constraints that are actually restraints very often, and cannot be chosen or ignored by individuals working within them. But there are models of organizations that can get around this problem.

One of them, curiously, is the British Army. Despite, on the face of it, being unusually hierarchical and tightly constrained by formal discipline and external restraints, the organizational model of the army is closer to the theater than you might expect. The core activity of the organization, the actual running about and blowing things up, is in the hands of the platoon under a platoon commander. In size and in terms of the relations within it, this organizational unit is very close to a theater ensemble under a director. There are high levels of trust and mutuality. There is a discipline of acceptance and energetic commitment to the constraints set by the director/ commander in the field, and there is a high tolerance for risk-taking.

While there is a disciplined respect for rank in the British Army, there is also an ability to drop the status game when required and enter into a fully, co-creative conversation when necessary. Because relative rank is so clear and so readily accepted by all, it is easy to drop it and then pick it up again, in very much the same way as a theater director does (this is particularly so in special forces, where creative imagination and an ability to improvise together are among their most important military assets). Army commanders do not have to fight for status within their team from day to day and the inflexible rigidity of command and control is long gone.

In the field they are also managed with a version of creative constraints called the Combat Estimate. This is in the form of seven questions that help a commander in the field to frame the constraints he or she will need to communicate in order to achieve the required objectives. The objectives are framed in the form of actions and effects rather than targets, and described with transitive verbs such as to unhinge, to surprise, to deceive, to pursue. An area may be required to be suppressed, or neutralized. These words are different and have quite specific and clearly understood meanings. How the action is accomplished, and what resources are needed and over what time frame, is allowed to emerge from the efforts of the fighting unit. The commanders are there to observe what is emerging, support the unit's efforts and reframe the objectives as the situation unfolds. Many successful organizations have elements of these structures and they do seem, in some cases, to yield consistently good results.

In the end, the problem of risk is one of managing for unexpected outcomes. Mitigating risk is partly to do with managing in a way that reduces the probability of unexpected outcomes, but it is also about being sufficiently responsive and adaptable to take advantage of what happens to happen. In *art* we are looking to set up complex emergent scenarios in which we are hoping to get unexpected outcomes – at least some of the time. We strive to create the circumstances in which we might be struck by an insight. Once we are, we proceed to go along with it, explore it, allow it to lead us somewhere and then intervene to stop it, or delete it, or adjust it to the direction we desire for our work. We choose and select from what happens to happen and make our work from that.

CHAPTER 15

Why Artists Should Rule the World

Works of art are the traces that artists leave behind them as they pursue their obsessions. Artists therefore, do not view their works in the way that others do. They are not the end of the activity; art is in the action, the endless process of practice and creation. Artists are artisans first. They are practical craftspeople and the arts have at their heart a core of knowledge that is not merely cognitive but physically embedded in the whole person. This type of knowledge can only be acquired by practice and is best transmitted by experience – you cannot learn how to be a classical guitarist, or a painter only by reading a book. Becoming an artist is a physical experience.

Artists, like many scientists, are engaged on an open-ended journey of discovery. They seldom, therefore, spend time reflecting on what they do in the abstract and there is not much written by artists on their creative processes (Ghiselin 1952). But the arts represent a body of knowledge that is profoundly useful to society, not only in the content of finished works, but also in the skills, practices and disciplines of artists themselves. The marginalization of the skills of making art, in education and in everyday life, are depriving us of a wealth of principles and approaches to thinking and doing that have, I believe, the power to transform the way we approach the management of our whole society. This book is about directing creativity. It is about initiating and sustaining creative activity in people and giving that endeavor a direction. It is also about trying to establish a way of shaping what we do and what we make, to a moral and aesthetic end. Artists do not just want to make things that people will buy. They also try to make things that are beautiful and true.

There is a popular misconception that artists are chaotic and eccentric people. They are not. They merely operate a conceptual framework that is different from that inhabited by those who are not artists but is equally rigorous and systematic.

Eccentric means off-center – away from the center. Artists are that; they need to be on the margin to find ideas and they need to tolerate chaos because there is a place between "what has been" and "what is becoming" that is chaotic. Without visiting that place they are not innovating. There is also a widespread fallacy that these differing conceptual frameworks are in some way competing; that the truths of art are in some way inferior to the truths of science. This is dangerous nonsense. We need, and daily use, a multitude of frames to make sense of the world and to navigate through it successfully. Familiarity with many different ones only serves to make us wise (Midgley 1985, 1989, 2001).

Business is a creative act. It too is about making things. It is where thought, imagination, ethical and aesthetic judgment connect with the process of making things; it varies in emphasis with the making of art and the making of science and the making of the world but there is no fundamental separation between these activities. There are no "two cultures" of art and science, in some way opposed or competing. Whatever we are making, we draw on the same faculties; imagination, judgment, and action. Scientists do not work without recourse to their imagination; artists do not create without hours of meticulous, repetitive, work.

There does seem to be, however, some kind of split in worldview between the doggedly materialistic and the rest. In declaring that "there is no alternative" to free-market capitalism, for instance, we are endowing what is only the sum of our conscious acts with a power like that of a Newtonian law of mechanics.

We are increasingly told to regard ourselves as if we were bundles of inert processes at the mercy of the immutable laws of the free market, or the swish of our chemical juices.

These descriptions are dangerous. Tell us we are selfish gene-machines, that fanatical competitiveness is all there is, and it will become so. We are always in the process of evolving. Everything we are, and everything we do, is a draft, a rehearsal, so there are always bits that do not fit, that seem left over or extraneous or just plain wrong, things that are not ideal or appropriate. We are not completed, our natures are not finished, nor can we ever be. This transitional space – the work in progress – half in the head and half in the world – is a very odd place to be.

The problem of giraffeness

But the truth is that all organic life is constantly in this emergent, uncompleted place. Giraffes look odd because they are odd. They are not "finished:" they are on their way somewhere else. Their legs are too long and so are their necks. They are a "mistake," a draft, a sketch. They are not the correct and final answer to the questions of giraffeness, they are a temporary solution. In a few million years they will look completely different (if they have not been entirely erased from the picture). And everything else in the natural world is like this too. We are not God's perfect final creation, we are weird and wonderful transitional forms and we will continue to shape-shift and evolve and transform as long as there is life on Earth. The problem of natural selection and evolution is not "How did something as perfect as the eye come about?" It is, rather, "Where on Earth is this odd organ going?" (Midgely 1985, 1981; Dawkins 1989; Goodwin 1994).

The creative process in nature, in art and in the world is about this dynamic, transitional place – and it is about choosing. Democracy is not the perfect final word in world government. The American constitution, with its many amendments, is a transitional work in progress, and so is democracy, so is the "free" market. But unlike nature we can do something about whether some of its manifestations exist. Unlike in natural selection, where the direction of evolution is essentially controlled by what happens to happen, we are the selectors, the designers and directors of this human creation. We can amend the constitution; we can change the rules by which capitalism operates. We are not at the mercy of the gods in these matters, or any other matters. Increasingly it is the case that everything is at the mercy of us. We *are* the architects of our own destiny and, increasingly, of everything else's as well. What we are suffering from is a lack of imagination and lack of a metaphor to help us regain control of our collective destiny and give us a map with which to navigate the future.

The maps we have used until recently are old. The dominant ones in the West come mostly from the machine age, the mechanical thinking that transformed nineteenth-century agriculture and industry. But we are resoundingly out of the mechanical age. We have indisputably mastered mechanics and engineering and have the means to alter our environment and provide for all our needs. We probably even have the technology to do it sustainably and fairly for the whole planet. We do not however seem to have the will. This very desire for direction and control is itself discredited. The failure of communism to produce prosperity or happiness, the terrible carnage unleashed by dictators, has made even the aspiration to direct things on the grand scale, a suspect project.

Leading with a misty vision

It seems to be a fact that social systems need connectedness and people need a degree of free choice, however limited, for creativity and change to emerge in a way that allows for the possibility of improvement. At its crudest level, this is what politics and economics are all about. Too much of the wrong sort of control and the system ossifies, becomes bureaucratic or tyrannical, too little and it becomes arbitrary and chaotic, massively rewarding some at terrible cost to others. What we are looking for is a process for directing the creativity of complex systems with the right balance between control and freedom, between order and chaos, between clarity and mist, between fecundity and death. Managing these paradoxical forces is what artists do.

We *can* direct social change, not by engineering but by art, by imagining better futures and equipping people with the skills to make these visions manifest. Artists know that in making a vision manifest it will change and adapt. Paintings, books and plays are made – they are not designed and implemented. Along the way there is room for continual adaptation, openness to the continuous possibility of a better manifestation of the vision. Choice exists. And in the collaborative arts is a wealth if skills, practices and tacit knowledge for performing this balancing act.

Revolutionary movements usually proceed by attempting to sweep away what is there and start afresh. But in art there is never really a blank canvas. To an observer of the arts, it may look as if a new work or movement has exploded onto the scene from nowhere, or more usually, we are told, from the unique mind of some lonely genius. But artists know that their work is always connected to what has gone before. The path to innovation begins in the past. When we are creating things we are always starting from somewhere; the contents of our heads, the preconceptions of our audience, the constraints of our chosen medium. Art is made from other art.

Artists achieve their original results by daring interventions that open out the possibilities that increase complexity rather than limit it. This inspired guessing and framing of imaginative questions is actually how research scientists proceed as well, but they bury this fact in their conclusions. Like artists, they publish only the finished result; they do not publish all the failed guesses, the rehearsals, the experiments that went wrong. The interventions creative people make, may not lead the emerging work in entirely the right direction at a stroke, but they will bias it in a certain direction and the effect of the intervention will be to generate possibilities that cannot be conceived until the intervention has taken place and the system begins to move in a new direction.

Fear that this process will be opening us to "unforeseen consequences" prevents us taking radical action. But unforeseen consequences are exactly what we are looking for if we are being creative. If they are unforeseen they are much more likely to be original and new. In creating a work of art, the artist is continually selecting from the ideas that emerge from the creative process. The artist will make an intervention and let it run a while and then choose whether to leave it, or stop it, or add another intervention that has been suggested by the first. They are constantly vigilant and constantly engaged with the work as it unfolds.

Keeping God out of the picture

This process is very like the evolution by selection that Darwin (1998) talks about in *On the Origin of Species* – the selection by the farmer, or animal breeder that chooses which lines will survive in his stock. In nature, as in farming, this selection process operates only in the here and now; it does not operate in the past or in the future. The difference between the human activity and the "natural" selection that Darwin talks about is that in farming (or in art) someone looks at what is there in front of them and chooses; in nature the choosing is not done by man.

In nature, the "choices" are a result of the complex interaction of organisms going about their daily lives. Eating, breeding, dying, raising their offspring, falling ill and getting better, and the shape of present creation is only the incidental result of this activity over time. We can look at the trace it leaves in fossils and imagine we see a journey of development, but the selection mechanism that produces this development has no plan and does not "choose" with any intent, or with any design of how the world should be in the future, or any regard for how it was in the past.

In art the selection process is directed by the conscious choices of the artist: "I will add some blue here;" "I'll leave that bit alone;" "I'll rewrite this sentence and change that metaphor;" "I think this bit is finished now." The creative process in art is parallel to creativity in nature. It is open and emergent and complex and it takes time, but it is constrained by the practicalities of the medium and the imagination of the artist, and it is shaped by the artist's conscious choices. Unlike Darwin's evolution by natural selection, it can be encouraged to unfold in a direction that the artist chooses. Art is about allowing creativity, emergence, and evolution to happen, but giving it direction, shape; it is about making choices and directing the emergent flow of creativity in a particular way.

In business and increasingly in politics, people talk as if they are subject to the same process as Darwinian natural selection, that they are at the mercy of "market forces," that they have no choice. While there are ways in which all social interactions are subject to a process like evolution, in that some enterprises become "successful" and some ideas "dominant," that selection is not "natural" in the sense that Darwin meant.

People talk as if "the market" were a person: it has "unseen hands" and "sentiments" and it "decides" things. People also talk as if it were a force of nature, like the weather or gravity, something over which people can exercise no control. In fact, if you put these two ideas together, you can say that people talk about the market as if it were a god: a powerful, sentient thing, separate from us, whom we must obey if we are to survive. What we are struggling to name here is a capacity for creativity that seems to be inherent within the system of the free market, a creative property of the market itself that does not just reside in the creativity of the individual people that make up the market (Bronk 1998).

Darwin also had this problem when he tried to describe the action of "natural" selection – the phenomenon that gives direction to the creative activity of nature. He ends up talking as if "natural selection" were some kind of deity as well:

> It may metaphorically be said that natural selection is daily and hourly scrutinising, throughout the world, the slightest variations; rejecting those that are bad, preserving and adding up those that are good; silently and insensibly working, wherever and whenever opportunity offers.

"The market" does seem, on the face of it, to operate like this; like a creative or destructive force of nature; silently and insensibly selecting from the variety of human production those things that will survive. But Darwin goes on to describe the goal of all this scrutinizing and rejecting, thus:

> silently and insensibly working at the improvement of each organic being in relation to its organic and inorganic conditions of life.

Here is the fundamental difference. The market is made of people like you and me and they are not "insensibly working"; they know exactly what they are doing and they are not working "at the improvement of each organic being in relation to its conditions of life" – they are noisily and consciously working to make as much money for themselves as they can (Frank 2001).

People – not "market forces" – make judgments and exercise choices and thus give direction to the creative activity of the entire business world. The market is not a natural force. It is a human agency, it is a thing we have made, and one of its driving principles is human selfishness. This bald truth about commerce, however, has been given an entirely spurious dignity by an element of the scientific community who argue that *every* act is "really" an act of selfishness and that natural selection as described by Darwin is not a result of some inherent creative property of complex dynamic systems, but comes about by the competing selfishness of all living things squabbling for resources.

The selfishness myth

This wretched idea that started with Hobbes and has been revitalized by Richard Dawkins and others has really muddied the water. It seems to imply that the direction of all creativity in nature is defined by this force of selfishness. A superficial look at Dawkins or others of his ilk makes it look as if they are saying that genes can have motives and their motive is selfishness and that they control our actions as if we were machines designed only to carry these pesky creatures around – so that even when we rescue a total stranger from a rising flood, or feel revulsion at the idea of someone abusing a child, we are "really" only being selfish. Apart from the bizarre idea that a string of molecules can have desires, this notion has got into our thinking, in the same way that Huxley's unintended bowdlerization of Darwin got us into a debate about God (Dawkins might call this dangerous misconception a meme) (Dawkins 1989).

The problem with this myth of the selfish gene is that it has given a spurious scientific credibility to the operation of free markets. It makes it look as if "market forces" are a result of some ungovernable natural force of selfishness that is embedded in our DNA. So the "free market" becomes the only real, true, honest, place to operate because it's all about selfishness, and selfishness is not only natural, it is the prime mover of all our actions and we are genetically programed to be selfish, so there is no alternative to a free market. Science has "proved" it.

This self-serving argument is not at all surprising when you consider that Darwin, when trying to describe the phenomenon he observed in nature and labeled "natural selection," found elements of his conceptual framework in the Dismal Science and leaned heavily on Malthus, Adam Smith and other writers, who were passionate advocates of free-market capitalism. But the fact that gets left out of these discussions of motivations and selfish *actions* is the one that artists live with all the time. It is the fact that the actions we do *not* take have consequences too. The whole language of motives, whether "selfish" or "altruistic," is dangerously misleading because what turns out to happen in the real world is not just the consequence of our conscious, or even unconscious, actions and intentions. What happens in the real world is also shaped by the things we do *not* do and do *not* intend. Our "non-actions" have consequences too.

Talking about motivations, however metaphorically, simply does not help us to understand the phenomenon.

The influence of sleeping lions

There is a strong sense in which creativity in art is a process of revelation as much as it is one of creation. The first acts, the first choices an artist makes set up parameters for the work. They define the creative field; within that field there are then an infinite number of possibilities. Even if the field is tightly defined there are still an infinite number of possibilities within it; the world is fractal. As soon as any action is taken, a sentence written, a character imagined, the field changes and another set of possibilities are generated. The creative act is, to a great extent, about choosing between this infinite number of possibilities and, by those choices, generating more. But whenever we make a choice to do something, we are also deciding not to make manifest the myriad other choices that every act begins to bring into existence.

When lions are sleeping they are affecting the evolution of gazelles exactly as much as they do when they are awake and chasing them. Their connection to the evolution of the gazelle is not defined by their motives – selfish or otherwise – it is defined by the whole consequence of all their actions and non-actions from moment to moment. It is influenced by their whole "presence" in the ecosystem, not by any one motive they may have or by any one action or group of actions they may take. In the lab, if you do not add the heat then the gas stays the same, it does not expand. Doing nothing has no consequences for the gas. In the savanna, if you do not chase the gazelle then it has time to feed or give birth unmolested. If you do not do the weeding, an English garden does not stay the same; given enough neglect, it turns into a forest. If you make no effort to be nice, people may grow to hate you. In the real world our non-actions have enormous consequences.

This is a very worrying idea. It is so worrying that we block it out almost entirely from our thinking. I would be quite mad to spend time worrying about the consequences of the fact that I do not live in California or Trincomalee, but the fact that I do not does have consequences. The absence of my ways, ideas, spending power, children, and so on are absences that contribute to the shape those places take. I could be there. If I was, then in a tiny way they would be different. The fact that I choose not to go, in a tiny way, shapes how those places are. We feel this when we leave the house at six a.m. to go to work, knowing that we will not see our children again till they are asleep, but we do not dwell too long on the consequences of our absence from our children's lives, because we are doing something else for them that preoccupies us.

"Author, Author!!"

Artists are in a different position. When a novelist is sitting thinking about a scene they are to write, say, the scene alluded to above – the parent leaving the house to go to work – they may decide to make the character stay; and to imagine how life unfolds that day. And they find themselves in an alternative world, as rich with possibilities, good and bad, as any other. They are continually making complex, imaginary experiments, playing with the magical "What if …?" and choosing between the results. Artists know the world is an infinitely complex place, and there are infinite possibilities and infinite numbers of causes for them and they know how to operate there. Why do we allow "the market" to be the author of our works? Why don't we do something else? Why don't we give the creativity of business a different direction? Because, unlike the natural world, the creativity and abundance of commerce *is* to a large extent directed by individual selfishness, though it doesn't have to be.

Selfishness is not the originator of creative abundance. Creative abundance is a byproduct of complexity – but unlike the pointless beauty and diversity of the natural world that has unfolded without intention, the form of the human world *is* shaped to a large degree by selfishness – and that we can change. Whatever their effects in the world, artworks have an author; the directing intelligence is named and known and can be cross-examined and held to account, as it can with the published work of scientists. With the effects of the works of business this is less easy to do. Whose idea was it that cars should be fast, sexy, heavily polluting, and wasteful of petrol? Who decided that mechanically recovered meat products were a good idea? Who made us all suddenly start wearing nylon in the 1960s and then stop in the 1970s? Who is responsible for global warming? These products of business and industry have all been made by people, operating in ways not wildly different from that of any other person who makes things, but there is a problem of authorship. And consequently there is a problem of who is responsible for whether they are good or bad.

When the phenomena are obviously and seriously dangerous, like cigarettes or drugs with dangerous side effects, there is sometimes a legal attempt to pin blame and these attempts are increasingly successful. They increasingly confirm that there are authors. But it is often a long struggle to get this level of accountability established and there is a genuine sense that, in the case of something dangerous or bad, pinning responsibility on one or two individuals is still not quite fair. The bad consequences of business activity are the result of actions that were dictated by "market forces." The perpetrators were in some sense "only obeying orders." And yet businesses are desperately keen to claim authorship of the good bits, patenting and defending intellectual property with great vigour.

In the theater there is also a problem of authorship. Directors, writers and actors collaborate and the end product is a joint endeavor, but authorship is known. In spite of the emergent qualities of the collaborative process, it is still possible for the director of the enterprise to give the work its final shape. The writer, the actors, and the director are all named on the poster; they are ultimately responsible for how it turns out. There seems to be a belief in business, however, that many of the products and the results of business activity have come about, at least in part, as a result of "market forces;" that many of the judgments that control the direction of creative activity in business are made not by people but by "the market" People in business far too easily abdicate responsibility for the choices they make. And I include myself in this.

Democratic governments, it could be said, do have at their heart "the improvement of each organic being in relation to its conditions of life." They set up regulations and enact laws that have the general good as their guiding principle, rather than individual selfishness, and they ameliorate the evil consequences of the unregulated "free market" a bit. But here something odd happens. If we have too many laws and regulations, they seem to stifle creativity. The energy and innovation of industry and commerce seems to dry up and stagnate. And if we have too few, the sanctioned selfishness that is the tacit moral order of the free market, produces inequality, exploitation and environmental degradation. How do we give the creativity of business and industry a direction that better serves the interest of the whole of organic life, without stifling its extraordinary energy and power?

Physics also proceeds by limiting possibilities, by trying the almost impossible task of generating a field within which to create where there are only one or two possibilities. With huge effort and enormous resources, it is possible to create these bizarre and unnatural places. You can construct a place in which there is no air and you can examine the properties of a pure gas and decide on causality. But these are completely unnatural places. What applies there never applies, in that simple way, in nature. In nature there are always an infinite number of other influences and contingent facts that mean the simple, direct, causal relationships do not operate. And yet it is science we turn to for models of how to operate in the infinitely complex world.

Art starts with an assumption of complexity. On whatever scale you look at the world, it is impossible not to see that it is infinitely complex.

Art proceeds by making choices – nudging the complex whole in a particular direction, adding bits on and leaving bits alone as they proceed, until the whole thing takes on a shape and form that the artist can identify as finished. In a very odd but real sense the creative process in the arts could be described as collaboration between the artist and the materials with which they work.

Since the industrial revolution, art has become beleaguered. Artists and their special styles of thought and ways of working have been steadily marginalized. A mythology has grown up around them, to do with genius and inspiration and intuition. Science has won the field as dominant thought-style and owner of the truth. But now we need art back. We need artists because their methods are as coherent, as rational and as practical as science and they may provide a way of dealing with this core problem of directing the creativity of commerce. Business is a creative process like art, not a creative process like science; it does not take place in a laboratory where complexity can be controlled.

In human affairs, our will, our judgment, our taste is always present. We can decide we do not like the way things are going and stop them. We can decide tomorrow that we will make the trading of shares illegal and utterly change the way capitalism functions. We can decide to enforce climate legislation or ban GM food. We can choose to wage war over oil or we can choose not to. The problem we have is that because we prefer to trust science-thinking rather than arts-thinking, we are constantly surprised by the fact that what emerges when we exercise our choice can be unexpected or unforeseen. This emergence is what artists revel in: it is creativity, and this phenomenon is what artists know how to handle. And while we have got as far as recognizing the creative potential of complex dynamic systems, we have not yet developed the skills to direct that creativity without suffocating it; we still think and act like nineteenth-century engineers.

People in business need to concern themselves with truth and beauty and goodness as well as with profit. And they need to wrestle authorship away from the myth of the market and its secret selfishness and begin to direct things like a great artist does – steering the extraordinary, unfolding process of making things, towards results that are good, beautiful, true and profitable. Because one of the many myths that has grown up around the arts is that great artists never make money. They often do.

Donald Rumsfeld – a cautionary tale

In April 2003 Donald Rumsfeld, then secretary of state for defense, gave his famous response to a question from the press about looting in

Iraq: "Stuff happens!" This was not just a truism about the consequences of his strategy but also very revealing about his view of strategy for the whole invasion. At the same press conference, he also said: "The plan is a complex set of conclusions or ideas that then have a whole series of alternative excursions that one can do, depending on what happens ..."

This is how artists work. They begin by making an intervention of a kind that has a visionary motivation but only patchy detail about the end result. Their first interventions are, also, often small-scale but audacious. Unlike (one would hope) military leaders, artists are trying to set up multiple, complex reactions, they are trying to release the potential of the given situation, reveal its hidden complexity.

Artists make an intervention and then see what it does. They live with it on the paper, in the rehearsal room, examine and reflect on it, then make another. It is an iterative process. Watching painters or theater directors at work, you see that they spend long hours just looking, considering, letting the implications of the intervention they have made sink in. Artists work by layering up, increasing the complexity of the confined moment in order to generate possibilities for its final expression.

The creative process feels like midwifery – facilitating the birth of a thing that in some sense already exists but is not yet in the world. Both creating it and aiding its birth. In theater this process feels as if you are leading the ensemble towards a misty vision. Elements of the goal are clear – some telling detail or some mood, or some passionately held belief; but the manifestation must be found out there, in the stuff that happens in the rehearsal room. The best directors create their work from what is happening in front of them. And there is a subtle relationship between, on the one hand, being led by the stuff that happens and, on the other, nudging that stuff in a particular direction by your interventions.

The difference with Rumsfeld is that artists have the work's best interests at heart. They want it to be beautiful and true, and also self-consistent – true to itself as a work. Therefore they are vigilant for the results of each intervention and are prepared to be influenced by them. They balance emergent serendipity, the stuff that happens to happen, with their vision for the end result.

An intervention having occurred, and a creative chaos having been set up (because it is creative as well as shockingly destructive), what is being made in Iraq from the blood of the participants is not knowable. Great artists maintain a fine balance between what something is and what it could become, letting the work in progress speak to them as they work on. They allow a work to become what it is, not what the artist wants it to be – a darker "Hamlet" than they expected, a more shocking portrait than they anticipated, a sadder book than they set out to write. But that is because artists are amoral. The judgments of artists are finally, only matters of opinion – it delights me, it bores you. Art in this sense doesn't matter at all.

But great artists are also masters of their craft. They have a profound embodied knowledge of the medium they are working in. They know its complexities and their own limitations in it. They are rigorous and they are consistent and they understand the power of setting the right constraints. They know what to eliminate; what to finally exclude. They move on by selecting, ruthlessly, from what emerges, the constraints that will define the next phase of the work. They never go back. They cut, they edit and they overpaint. They understand that if you are doing art and not engineering then your actions will produce stuff and the stuff will have in it fragments of the next phase of the work and you must find those fragments, reveal them, encourage them and add to them, and then see what you have got: pause, consider, look, meditate and then act again.

Great artists journey in to this chaotic place and maintain their vision. They have, in Keats's words, "negative capability" – an ability to maintain themselves in this place and keep their judgment. They continue to nudge what is, towards their desired goal. They do not become overwhelmed. What Rumsfeld set up in Iraq was an artistic process, not a military or a political one; he and his cohorts were dreamers, fantasists. But artists generally stick to art, where they can work in this way and do no harm. Spilt paint is not a problem like spilt blood. An intervention that leads nowhere can be abandoned, over-painted or torn up.
Rumsfeld:

> This is fascinating. This is just fascinating. From the very beginning, we were convinced that we would succeed, and that means that that regime would end. And we were convinced that as we went from the end of that regime to something other than that regime, there would be a period of transition. And, you cannot do everything instantaneously; it's never been done, everything instantaneously …

> And, you say, 'Well, what was it in the plan?' The plan is a complex set of conclusions or ideas that then have a whole series of alternative excursions that one can do, depending on what happens. And, they have been doing that as they've been going along. And, they've been doing a darn good job.

> Think what's happened in our cities when we've had riots, and problems, and looting. Stuff happens! But in terms of what's going on in that country, it is a fundamental misunderstanding to see those images over, and over, and over again of some boy walking out with a vase and say, 'Oh, my goodness,

you didn't have a plan.' That's nonsense. They know what they're doing, and they're doing a terrific job. And it's untidy, and freedom's untidy, and free people are free to make mistakes and commit crimes and do bad things. They're also free to live their lives and do wonderful things, and that's what's going to happen here. (Donald Rumsfeld, April 2003; transcript courtesy of the US Department of Defense)

Astonishingly, what Rumsfeld seems to be saying is that the entire invasion was based on an idea about "freedom" that he had. He then proceeded to explore that idea in a way that an artist would recognize, dabbling, experimenting, trying things out, making rough sketches, but proceeding without any skill or experience of the materials. The "materials" in this case were the lives (and history) of the Iraqi people and the physical fabric of their nation. The audacity of this is utterly breathtaking.

The interesting thing is that he clearly must have thought that, by pursuing an idea about "freedom," "order" would somehow follow. That the driving force of constructive, creative emergence is "freedom." Every artist knows that the opposite is true. Creativity is a boundary phenomenon. It demands constraints to be set, or what emerges cannot be given direction and shaped to the artist's ends. Civilization, like the art that represents it, is dependent on constraint, not freedom. Or rather it is based on a complex and delicate balance between the two, a balance which has taken thousands of years to perfect and takes hourly and daily effort to maintain.

What is happening slowly in Iraq is that the people are beginning to set their own boundaries and constraints, forming alliances, creating boundaries between themselves and other groups and along these boundaries the new form will begin to take shape. Ironically this Iraq will, painfully, be made, freely, by its people but it may finally take a form that that bears no resemblance whatever, to the dreams in Donald Rumsfeld's head. There may be the possibility of nudging what is emerging in Iraq to something that is good and beautiful and true and self-consistent, but it will require the amoral pragmatism of a visionary artist.

At its most basic level, someone has to draft and enforce some laws: but just as important, they have to convince the ensemble that those constraints are ones that they are excited about performing within. Someone must set them, or else they will emerge, from the unstoppable metamorphosis of any complex dynamic system, from the stuff that happens to happen. Iraq at the time of writing is sliding into civil war. This will generate more constraints to which the actors in the theater of this war will respond with energy and imagination. The original directors of this drama are no longer in control – the actors are improvising a new performance of their own. What, in the end, they create may appall the original directors of the project.

Applying constraints is an act of power. But artists don't see them as that. They are constraining but they are not felt to be such. They are selected and chosen because they feel inspiring, not constraining. When they are chosen and applied by the artist themselves – "I will only use shades of blue in this picture" – they may hit the artist with a surge of excitement and euphoria. "Aha, that's the answer!" they may feel – "Just using blue will allow me to express what I want." Along the way, that will throw up technical problems which will check the creative flow until another idea releases the artist forwards. The theater director formulates constraints of this sort for others. The business manager needs to find a way to do the same for his staff to release them into creative working.

This brings us to the deeper ethical question. If you are to direct an enterprise, what are the principles, the moral framework, by which you judge what choices to make and what constraints to put in place? In business the explicit agenda is profit and probably personal gain. If these values are allowed free rein and constraints are set by these criteria, we get what one would expect. Those with the authority to set and police the constraints create a world in which they gain profit and have huge personal gain. However, as some sectors of commerce become more creative and begin to adopt the artistic paradigm in their search for novelty and innovation, they are, increasingly, including the customers in their creative ensemble.

But this undermines the tacit assumption of capitalism. If we are genuinely co-creating, what is the proposition we are investigating, and to what end? Who will finally benefit from our work and in what way? Control of the form of what is being created in some sectors of the economy is slipping out of the hands of the capitalists, in the same way that control of the direction of Iraq has slipped out of the hands of the invaders. Depending on whose side you are on, this is either a disaster or a very welcome change. Creative leadership requires that we are explicit about our fundamental desires for the project and that if we are going to direct it, we need to be completely open about our beliefs and explicit about our visions for what we hope might unfold. We then need to be sure that we have the full authority and consent to set these constraints for others.

Ruskin's question

Until very recently, artists have had very little to do with business. It is one of those non-actions that have profound consequences. The absence of artists and their ways from the ecology of business has meant that there has grown up a tangled thicket of misunderstanding about how artists actually do work and a huge literature of management theory, most of which seems to be based on how scientists, soldiers or engineers work. What artists do is set up an emergent creative process and then they nudge it in the direction they want. Creativity, in nature, in art and in science, is about stimulating growth and then selecting from the results; it's more like gardening than anything else.

Painters and writers share a common moan about the fear of the empty page. There is the blank canvas, the "tabula rasa." There is nothing out there in the world. But the fear of the blank page is not really an anxiety about having no ideas: it is an anxiety about how to start; how to invade this empty space with your first, terrible, inadequate, gesture. Before you take action, there are only your thoughts, your ideas, your visions, jumbled about in the cave of your head. But of course that is quite a lot. The real problem is, actually, how do you start this piece of work?

You start by making a mistake – a mark, a sentence, a brush stroke and you have begun; it will always be a "mistake," it will rarely survive to the end of the creative arc. But as soon as you have made even the most tentative start, you have changed the nature of the problem and that action helps to constrain and define the next, and so on. As you progress, that thing you are creating becomes more and more complex until it begins to have emergent properties and then the task becomes more one of selection than of invention. Ideas begin to emerge from the work in hand rather than just from your imagination. The possibilities become increasingly shaped by what has been done so far. You are in the flow.

In a collaborative art, like theater, these processes are more visible than in other forms. Many have been distilled into processes and techniques that are readily accessible and are transferable to other situations. But behind them is the fundamental judgment of choosing from the many possibilities, and, in the end, the person that makes those choices is responsible for them and their consequences – so they need to be made wisely.

What I am advocating here is to open up our understanding and our thinking to the ways of artists; to understand what this generative, creative process is, both in nature and in the human world (for they are the same phenomenon) and to use this understanding to reclaim the idea of authorship, of authority: to be the directors of these processes in the world and to articulate exactly what it is that we profess.

"Profess" is an archaic word. It not only means what we pretend to think and feel, but it can also mean what we have faith in, what we believe in. It is also the root of the word professional. If we are to direct things then we are going to be making judgments and those judgments will be based on our values, our beliefs, our tastes. We influence things by the choices we make and those choices are ours and we are responsible for them and for their consequences. Business is now a profession. But if we are to be professionals what do we profess to believe in? What are the values by which we will make our judgments when we set about the next phase of our work as artists in the world? The Victorian artist and critic John Ruskin put this question very forcefully in his collection of essays, *Unto This Last*, published in 1862:

Five great intellectual professions, relating to daily necessities of life, have hitherto existed – three exist necessarily in every civilized nation:

The Soldier's profession is to defend it.

The Pastor's is to teach it.

The Physician's to keep it in health.

The Lawyer's to enforce justice in it.

The Merchant's to provide for it.

And the duty of all these men is, on due occasion, to die for it.

"On due occasion," namely:–

The Soldier, rather than leave his post in battle.

The Physician, rather than leave his post in plague.

The Pastor rather than teach falsehood.

The Lawyer rather than countenance injustice.

The Merchant – what is his "due occasion" of death?

It is the main question for the merchant, as for all of us. For, truly, the man who does not know when to die does not know how to live.

I was asked some years ago to work with a group of business people on a three-day retreat. My given topic was "Passion". At first I struggled with the idea that there could be anything like passion in business. The idea that people should be expected to be "passionate" about retail banking or selling industrial adhesives seemed to me absurd. But as the day progressed and I explored the concept with the group, using theater techniques and exercises, trying out "passionate" passages from King Lear, it became clear that there was only one meaning of passion being expressed among these people: passion as desire. They talked about the things that they felt passionate about. For example, their children, deep-ocean sailing, books and of course, winning. But passion was not expressed in the religious sense – the sense of sacrifice used by Ruskin.

There may be nothing in commerce that is worth the ultimate sacrifice: But to be clear about what things are worth in this sense, in the fully human sense of "What and how much, am I giving up to have this?" "What may die in me, or in the world, if I pursue this course?" perhaps gives us a better frame within which to make our choices.

BIBLIOGRAPHY

Boal, A. *Games for Actors and Non-Actors*, trans. Jackson, A. (Routledge 1992).

Boal, A. *The Rainbow of Desire: The Boal Method of Theatre and Therapy*, trans. Jackson, A. (Routledge 1995).

Bronk, R. *Progress and the Invisible Hand: The Philosophy and Economics of Human Advance* (Warner 1998).

Darwin, C. *On the Origin of Species by Natural Selection* (Wordsworth 1998 [1859]).

Dawkins, R. *The Selfish Gene*, 2nd edn (Oxford University Press 1989).

Frank, T. *One Market Under God* (Secker & Warburg 2001).

Gell-Mann, M. *The Quark and The Jaguar: Adventures in the Simple and the Complex* (Little, Brown 1994).

Ghiselin, B. (ed.) *The Creative Process* (University of California Press 1952).

Gleik, J. *Chaos: Making a New Science* (Sphere 1987).

Goodwin, B. *How the Leopard Changed Its Spots: The Evolution of Complexity* (Weidenfeld & Nicolson 1994).

Hyde, L. *The Gift: Imagination and the Erotic Life of Property* (Vintage 1979).

Johnstone, K. *Impro: Improvisation and the Theatre* (Methuen 1979).

Mangham, I.L. and Overington, M.A. *Organizations as Theatre: A Social Psychology of Dramatic Appearances* (Wiley 1987).

Midgley, M. *Heart and Mind: The Varieties of Moral Experience* (Methuen 1981).

Midgley, M. *Evolution as a Religion: Strange Hopes and Stranger Fears* (Methuen 1985).

Midgley, M. *Wisdom Information and Wonder* (Routledge 1989).

Midgley, M. *Science and Poetry* (Routledge 2001).

Ruskin, J. "Unto This Last," in *Unto This Last and Other Writings* (Penguin Classics 1985 [1862]).

Sennett, R. *The Corrosion of Character* (Norton 1998).

Sennett, R. *The Culture of the New Capitalism* (Yale University Press 2006).

Shaw, P. *Changing Conversations in Organisations: A Complexity Approach to Change* (Routledge 2002).

Tannen, D. *You Just Don't Understand: Women and Men in Conversation.* (Virago 1991).

Whatmore, J. *Releasing Creativity* (Kogan Page 1999).

DATE DUE

Demco